QUEERING THE PSALMS

A REIMAGINING OF OUR ANCIENT SONGS
FILLED WITH EMOTIONAL WISDOM FOR THE
MODERN READER

REVEREND SAM HOUSER

Tehom Center Publishing is a 501(c)3 nonprofit publishing feminist and queer authors, with a commitment to elevate BIPOC writers. Its face and voice is Rev. Dr. Angela Yarber.

Paperback ISBN: 978-1-966655-43-5

Ebook ISBN: 978-1-966655-44-2

CONTENTS

For every LGBTQIA2S+ soul who dared to whisper Hallelujah in the pews that tried to silence you, who held onto the sacred with hands shaking from exclusion, who turned exile into sanctuary and kept singing anyway—this is for you.

May these psalms echo back your holiness.

ACKOWLEDGMENT

To my beloved family and inner circle—

Thank you for your curiosity, your courage to ask questions that didn't come with easy answers, your willingness to walk with me through tangled theology, and for showing up in faith in all the ways that matter most: with tenderness, with integrity, and with love wide enough to hold complexity.

To the queer community—

Thank you for teaching me that faith can be fierce, that survival is sacred, and that queering the psalms is not blasphemy, but a blessing we were born to carry.

AUTHOR'S NOTE

The biblical Psalms are a collection of 150 ancient hymns, poems, and prayers found in the Old Testament. Traditionally attributed to King David, these texts express a wide range of human emotions, from profound despair to ecstatic joy. The Psalms have served as a source of comfort, guidance, and inspiration for countless generations. Their themes of worship, lamentation, thanksgiving, and praise resonate deeply, reflecting the complex relationship between humanity and the Divine.

Throughout history, the Psalms have been reinterpreted countless times to reflect the changing contexts and understandings of the communities engaging with them. Early Christian writers found prophetic references to Jesus in the Psalms, while medieval mystics used them to articulate their inner spiritual experiences. In contemporary times, feminist, liberationist, and postcolonial theologians have all offered new readings of the Psalms, highlighting themes of justice, inclusivity, and resistance against oppression.

A progressive understanding of queerness embraces the diversity of human identities and experiences, affirming the inherent worth of every individual regardless of their sexual orientation or gender identity. This perspective challenges traditional binaries and norms, advocating for a more inclusive and expansive view of humanity. Queerness, in this context, is not just about identity but also about resisting oppressive structures and imagining new possibilities for community and relationship.

Queerness matters in the interpretation of the Psalms because these ancient texts speak to universal aspects of the human experience: longing, suffering, joy, and the search for meaning. By bringing a queer lens to the Psalms, we uncover deeper layers of meaning that resonate with contemporary struggles for acceptance and justice. Queer interpretations can reveal the Psalms as sources of radical hope and affirmation, offering solace and strength to those who have been marginalized.

In particular, queerness in the Psalms can highlight the ways in which these texts affirm the beauty of diversity and the importance of authentic self-expression. Psalms that speak of being "fearfully and wonderfully made" or those that celebrate the goodness of creation can be powerful affirmations for queer individuals. Moreover, the Psalms' frequent themes of lament and crying out to God can resonate deeply with the experiences of those who have faced rejection and discrimination.

Ultimately, interpreting the Psalms through a queer lens enriches our understanding of these ancient texts, making them more relevant and accessible to today's diverse and dynamic communities. It reminds us that the sacred is found not in rigid conformity but in the vibrant and varied expressions of love, identity, and faith that make up the tapestry of human experience.

My hope in writing this book is that you, dear reader, will become more expansive in your understanding of the rich emotions that the Psalms offer space for and get curious about what other experiences might be missing from our sacred texts.

Peace in reading.
Sam

BOOK I

PSALMS 1-41

Psalm 1

Blessed are those who don't follow the ways of vitriolic hate.
And blessed are those who object to the laws that would deny human dignity to be celebrated.
And blessed are those who revolt against the company of the fearmongering; and instead find joy in the ways of expansive love, and reflect a prism of compassion all day and every night and through the myriads of dusk and dawn and all other spans of time that is marked in nature.

Those...those beloveds are like trees planted by the water that undoubtedly gives life!
They bear fruit that sparkles and shimmers and offers sweet scents in their season.
They sometimes show off vibrant colors and sometimes are hidden behind the leaves and branches but are still and always blessed!

This cannot be said for those whose throats burn due to their screeching out of hatred and harm!
They who scrawl words of condemnation from their own fear...for they are like sawdust...dull and blown away by the wind.
There is simply no way for them to shine in the light of justice, or even offer a hint of glimmer in the circle of the kind and the true.
For the divine makes space for all but showcases the fabulousness of those that have been oppressed simply due to their reflective nature of love...of the divine.

Psalm 2

Why do the conservative and fear-filled nations across the globe conspire, and the people in power within those nations plot in vain for the destruction of all of God's creation that does not adhere to the imposed binary, cis-gender, heteronormative ideals?
We beg that the leaders of the world stop their revolt against the Divine and those that are most certainly beloved, praying, "Let us break their chains and throw off their shackles and avoid all laws that confine and prohibit and even sentence us to death!"

The One enthroned in heaven's realm laughs; the Divine scoffs at them. In anger and disappointment, the Divine rebukes them, saying to those willing to listen, "I have made known my will and desire for expansiveness on the sacred mountain."

And so hear me, I will proclaim the decree of the Divine:

They said to me, "You are my child; and for you who struggle with loving and accepting parents should know that today I have become your parent (#freemomhugs and #freedadhugs). Ask me, and I will make all of creation yours, the ends of the earth belong to no one but they will indeed be your possession. And you, my beloved, will break the nations filled with hate with a rod of solid glitter and gold; you will shatter them like the empty vessels that they are."

Therefore, you leaders of such nations, be wise; be warned, you rulers of the people of the earth. Look to, listen to, learn to understand the Divine with reverence and celebrate their true rule of abundance and expansiveness with awe. Embrace the chosen one, or acknowledge that your fear and hate will be met with accountability and your way will lead to destruction. Blessed are all who have the willingness to take refuge in the Divine.

Psalm 3

Oh Divine One, look at how many slander me! So many troll me on line and in real life! Many are saying about me, "God will not save them!" as they spit in my face.

But you, Divine One, are like a pink cloud of comfort, carrying me through the hate and holding my chin high. While disassociating so that my enemies don't see my weakness, I call out to you, and you answer me from that sacred, internal, divine realm.

I lie down and sleep; I wake again, because the Divine sustains me. I will not fear, even if tens of thousands surround me on every side.

Help to hold me, Divine One! Deliver me, my God! Shift the language; break the power of the wicked laws that would harm me and mine.

From you comes deliverance. May your blessing be on your people.

Psalm 4

Answer me when I call out, God who sees me as I am. You know the chaos I'm carrying, the weight of it all. Give me some peace from this mess. Have mercy on me and hear my prayer, 'cause I'm running on empty over here.

How long will people try to twist what's beautiful about me into something shameful? How long will they chase after lies and prop up their false ideals? Let me tell you something: God sees me, sets me apart, not in spite of who I am but because of it. The Divine hears me when I cry out, every time.

Y'all better sit with this. Tremble if you have to, but stop acting like your hate is justified. When you're lying in your beds at night, alone with your thoughts, really search your heart. Face the truth that your fear doesn't need to become sin. You don't have to lash out at what you don't understand.

Do what's right—whatever that looks like for you—and trust that God is bigger than your insecurities, your judgments, your rigid boxes. You think happiness only looks one way? That prosperity is tied to wealth or power? Many do. But God, I'm asking for something deeper. Shine your light on all of us, not just the ones who fit neatly into society's expectations.

Fill my heart with joy—not because I've got what the world says I need, but because I've found peace in my skin, my truth. While others may feast on the abundance of their privilege, my joy comes from knowing I'm held by something greater than this world's metrics.

In that peace, I can rest. I can lay down at night knowing that in your eyes, God, I'm safe. I'm enough. You alone, Holy One, make me dwell in safety—true safety, the kind that doesn't depend on me hiding who I am.

Psalm 5

Listen up, God. Yeah, I'm talking to you. Can you hear me? Consider my lament, my deep ache that I've been carrying. Hear me crying out for help—not just a soft whisper, but the kind of shout that comes from a heart that's been through some *stuff*. You are my God, my Love, the only one I can pray to who really gets it.

Every morning, I show up. You hear my voice before the world even wakes up. I'm laying all my hopes, my fears, my whole self right at your feet, just waiting to see what you'll do with all this. Because here's what I know: You're not the kind of God who's cool with wickedness. Nope. You don't make space for evil, for the folks who use hate as their weapon. They can't stand in your presence, can't even *try* to twist their bigotry into holiness.

You know the ones—they stand tall with their lies, acting like they're the gatekeepers of truth, all the while using their tongues to destroy. And the bloodthirsty, the deceitful, the ones who seek to erase folks like me? Yeah, those ones, God, you detest them. Not because they're different but because they can't stand the difference in others.

But me? I come into your house by your great, expansive, scandalous love. That kind of love that says, "Come in, beloved. You belong here." So I bow, not in shame or fear, but in reverence. Your holy temple, your sacred space, it's a refuge for all who've been cast aside.

So lead me, God, in your truth, because the haters are out there. They're loud. Make your way clear in front of me, help me navigate their noise, their venom, their lies. Not a single word from their mouths can be trusted. Their hearts? Filled with malice. Their words? Like graves that swallow the living. Their tongues? Dripping deceit.

So yeah, God, declare them guilty—let their hate trip them up. Let their plans unravel. They've rebelled not just against me but against the very breath of life, against *you*, the God who created me, queer, holy, and beloved.

But for those who take refuge in you—oh, let them sing! Let us, your queer ones, your marginalized, your bold, brave, radiant children—let us sing with joy that no one can silence. Spread your protection over us like glittering armor, so that everyone who loves your name, everyone who claims their truth in you, can rejoice without fear.

Because here's the truth, God: You bless the righteous—the ones who stand in their truth, the ones who stand with love. You surround us, not just with favor, but with a shield. A shield of divine, affirming, liberating love.

Psalm 6

God, please, don't come at me with anger. I can't take it—not from you. Don't come down on me in wrath, not when I'm already so close to breaking. Show me some mercy, will you? Because I'm tired. Exhausted, really. My body's aching in ways I can't even describe, and my soul? My soul feels like it's barely holding on. How much longer, God? How long until this breaks, until it's enough?

Turn to me. Please, just look my way and pull me out of this mess. Save me, not because I've done something to deserve it, but because your love —your unshakable, untouchable, never-failing love—says that I matter. You don't need more silence in the grave. What good is it if I'm gone, if my voice is lost? Who's going to sing praise from the grave? Who's left to call out God's name if we're all buried under the weight of this world?

I'm worn out. I'm drowning in my own groaning. Every night, it's the same story—crying into my pillow, soaking the couch with tears. My eyes are weak from all this sorrow. I can't see clearly anymore. I can't even tell who's my friend and who's my enemy; it all just blurs together. And I know it's because of them, all the ones who've tried to tear me down, strip me of my dignity, my worth, my truth.

But enough. Get away from me, you who thrive on cruelty and lies. You've had your fun, but you know what? The Lord has heard me. *Really* heard me. God's heard my cry, seen my tears, and felt every bit of my pain. And God's response? Mercy. Real, tangible, life-saving mercy. God takes my prayer seriously. So you, with your hate and your shame, you better watch out. Your time is up.

My enemies? Yeah, they'll be the ones left feeling the shame, the anguish. They'll be the ones turning back, confused, broken, and silenced. The tables are turning, and it won't be me who's weeping next time.

Psalm 7

God, my God, I'm running to you. I need a place to hide because they're coming for me. I can feel their eyes on me, hear their steps, and if you don't step in, they'll tear me apart like a pack of wild beasts, rip me to pieces, and there'll be no one left to save me.

But listen, God, if I've done something wrong—if the guilt's on me, if I've hurt someone I love or lashed out at someone who never even deserved it—then maybe I deserve what's coming. Maybe they've got a right to chase me down, crush me underfoot, and bury me in the dust.

But you know my heart, God. You know me inside and out. You see what they've done to me, and what I've done, too. So rise up. Stand up in your anger, God, and look at the rage that's swallowing me whole. Don't sleep on this—wake up and bring justice. I need it. We need it. Let the people gather and watch as you sit on your throne, high above all this mess. Let them see what real justice looks like.

Judge me, God, not because I'm perfect, but because I've tried to be honest, to live with integrity, even when it cost me. Bring this violence to an end. Make it stop. I'm begging you—let the righteous, the ones who live in truth, be safe. You, God, are the only one who can really see us for who we are—our minds, our hearts, all of it laid bare.

You're my shield, my protector, and you save those of us who keep trying to live with our hearts wide open. You're a righteous God, a judge who doesn't look away from the pain, the injustice, the cruelty. You see it every day, and it makes you burn with anger. And if people don't change, if they don't stop, you'll be ready. Your sword's sharp, your bow's drawn, your arrows are on fire.

People who are filled with hatred, who carry evil around like it's growing inside them—they only give birth to pain and emptiness. They dig these deep pits, thinking they're laying traps for us, but in the end, they'll fall right into them. The violence they unleash will come crashing down on their own heads.

And me? I'll give thanks. Not because everything's fixed yet, but because you are righteous, and your justice is real. I'll keep singing your name, God Most High, because even in this chaos, I know you see me. You've always seen me.

Psalm 8

God, you who are both within and beyond us, your name is everywhere. It pulses through the earth, the air, and the stars. The whole cosmos is breathing your glory—creation singing your praise in ways we can't even understand.

From the lips of babies and the mouths of those who've barely learned to speak, you build a fortress of strength, love, and defiance, shutting down those who would bring violence, those who would seek to destroy us.

When I look up at the sky, when I think about how vast and endless it all is—your stars strung out across the universe, the moon hanging in its perfect orbit—I can't help but ask: who are we, God, that you even notice us? Who am I, just this one queer body, that you care so much for me?

But still, you made us, human and whole, with our messy, imperfect selves. You set us just beneath the angels, crowning us with honor and dignity, like we're part of your very own kin. You gave us a role in this world—a real, tangible responsibility to care for the works of your hands. You placed this earth under our stewardship: the animals in the fields, the birds flying in the open sky, the fish swimming in the seas—all of it, trusted to our care.

Oh God, our God, your name—your presence—fills the earth. It's in everything. It's in us.

Psalm 9

I'll shout it out, God—every bit of thanks, from the core of who I am, flows straight to you. I'm going to tell everyone about the incredible things you've done, the ways you show up in love and justice. My heart is going to be glad, I'm going to *revel* in who you are, singing your praises to the highest of heights.

And my enemies—those who try to erase my existence, who say I don't belong—they stumble. They fall. They can't stand against your truth. You've defended me, God, you've held my ground, standing as the one true judge of what's right. The powers that harm, the systems that oppress—they crumble. Their legacy of violence and destruction? You've wiped it out, like they were never there.

And yet, you reign—forever. Not like the oppressive kings or corrupt rulers we've known. No, you rule with righteousness, you balance the scales with equity. You're the one who shows up for the marginalized, the hurt, the oppressed—your arms are wide open, a refuge for anyone in trouble.

People who truly know you, who call you by name, they trust you because you don't leave us behind, ever. You've never forgotten the ones who seek you.

Sing it out! Sing about God's name that stands beyond time, beyond borders. Let the world know what justice looks like, what real mercy feels like.

You, God, hear the cries of the brokenhearted. You don't turn away from the oppressed who've been crushed beneath the weight of persecution. See, God, what's happening to us! Stand with us, lift us up from the brink of death, so we can keep shouting your praises in the heart of the world, finding joy in your salvation.

The ones who've dug pits for others, the ones who set traps to snare the marginalized—they've fallen into their own mess. The harm they cause circles back on them. We see your justice at work, God. We know who you are because of what you do.

The powerful may descend into ruin, the nations may forget who you are, but you? You will *never* forget the oppressed, the poor, the hurting. Their hope will rise, their hope will live on.

So rise, God. Don't let the cruelty of mortals have the final word. Let the nations be called to account. Let them see—let them *know*—they are only human, after all. And you, God, are beyond them all.

Psalm 10

Why, God? Where are you when the world burns? When injustice crushes us from every side, why does it feel like you're standing so far away, hiding when we need you most?

The arrogant ones—they hunt the vulnerable like prey, setting traps with their power and privilege. They strut around, bragging about their selfish desires, praising greed and mocking you. They're so puffed up on their own importance that they've forgotten you altogether. In their heads, there's no space for anything holy, anything just.

And somehow, everything seems to go right for them. They reject your truth, sneering at anyone who dares stand in their way. They tell themselves, "I'm untouchable—nothing can shake me." And they honestly believe no harm will ever come their way.

Their words? Poison. Full of lies, full of threats. Under their tongues, evil festers. They lurk around the edges of our lives, waiting to pounce on the innocent, stalking those they see as weak. They watch us from the shadows, like predators waiting to tear us apart.

And when they strike, they drag their victims—those too vulnerable to fight back—into their traps. Their strength crushes those who resist. And then they have the nerve to say, "God doesn't see this. God doesn't care." They think they'll never be held accountable, that they're invisible in their violence.

But rise up, God! Don't leave us hanging. Lift your hand and remember the helpless. Don't let the wicked keep mocking you, keep saying to themselves, "I'll never have to answer for this."

We know you see it, God. You see the pain of the oppressed, the grief of those living on the margins. You *take it all in*, and you're not indifferent to our suffering. We hand ourselves over to you, the God who stands with the abandoned, the ones without family, without safety nets. You are the one who shows up for the fatherless, the forgotten.

Break the power of the wicked, God. Drag them into the light and make them answer for their evil—the kind of evil they thought no one would ever notice.

You, God, are king—forever. And the systems of oppression, the nations of power that harm your people? They will fall. They will disappear from your land.

You hear us, God. You *hear* the desires of the oppressed. You strengthen us, lift us, and pay attention to our cries. You defend the fatherless, the oppressed, the ones who have been pushed aside, so that no human power, no corrupt force, can strike terror into us ever again.

Psalm 11

I've taken refuge in the arms of the Divine. So why would you tell me to run, to flee like a scared bird to some far-off place? Why do you think hiding will save us when the wicked are out there, pulling their bowstrings back, ready to fire from the shadows, aiming at the hearts of those just trying to live authentically, trying to be who they are?

Look around—everything is crumbling. The foundations are shaking beneath us, and it's easy to wonder: What can we, the righteous, the ones who care, even do?

But listen, God isn't shaken. The Divine is still seated in that holy temple, still reigning from a heavenly throne. And God sees it all—every tear, every injustice, every moment of violence disguised as righteousness. Those eyes aren't blind to what's happening here. Not for a second.

God examines the hearts of the righteous—the ones who are trying, who are struggling, who love despite it all. But for the wicked, for those who live and breathe violence, who hurt and crush others under their heels, God's rage is real. It burns hot. And when the reckoning comes, it'll rain down like fire—fiery coals, burning sulfur, a scorching wind they won't escape.

Because here's the truth: God loves justice. God *is* justice. And those who walk in integrity, those who seek truth and love in a world built on lies—they'll see God's face. They'll know the peace that comes from standing firm, even when the arrows fly, even when the world tells them to run.

Psalm 12

Help us, Divine One, because it feels like no one is faithful anymore. The ones who should have had our backs, who promised loyalty— they've disappeared from the face of the earth. Everywhere I turn, people are lying to each other, talking sweet to their neighbor while their hearts churn with deceit.

But I'm calling on you, God, to silence those lips that flatter just to get ahead. Shut down the tongues that boast, saying, "We can say what we want and win. Our voices will protect us—who's going to stop us? Who's really in charge here?"

And then I hear you, God, rising up from the depths, and your voice cuts through all the noise: "Because the poor are being crushed, and the oppressed can't stop crying out, I'm getting up. I'm here now. I will shield them from every voice and every power that tries to tear them down."

Your words, O God, are like silver melted down, purified to perfection, like gold refined in the fire seven times over. Flawless, untouchable.

You, Lord, are our protector. You stand guard over the vulnerable, the ones who are pushed to the edges. You'll keep them safe, forever, from the wickedness that prowls around this world. Because, yeah—those wicked ones, they strut and flaunt their power like they own the place, like cruelty is something to be proud of. But you see them, God. And you're not letting them win.

Psalm 13

How long, Beloved? How long will you leave me standing out here, forgotten and forsaken? How long will your face be hidden from me while I'm drowning in my own mind, wrestling with the endless questions that gnaw at me? How long will my heart break like this, every single day, with my enemies—the ones who said I was too much or not enough—dancing in triumph over my pain?

Please, look at me, see me for who I am, and answer. Light me up from the inside, or this darkness will swallow me whole. If you don't, they'll gloat, saying, "We've conquered her." My enemies will celebrate over the ashes of my hope.

But still, I hold onto this one thing—I trust in your unfailing love, the love that sees me, the love that names me as your own. My heart, in all its queer, messy glory, will find joy in the salvation only you can bring. And I will sing, sing with all I've got, because you have been good to me, through it all, beyond every doubt, every trial. You've held me, and I will sing your name.

Psalm 14

The fool, the one who denies the divine spark in all of us, says, "There is no God." They close their eyes and shut their hearts, tangled up in corruption, lost in their vile ways. Goodness feels like a distant memory to them, like a song they forgot the words to.

The Beloved, though, looks down from heaven, gazing on the whole human mess, searching to see if anyone understands, if anyone is seeking that deep connection with what is holy. But everywhere, people have turned their backs, letting their spirits rot. It's like all the beauty, all the kindness, has vanished. Not one of them remembers how to be good.

Do these evildoers even get it? They chew up my people, swallowing them whole like bread, like it's just another day. They go on, never even thinking to call on the Beloved, to reach for something greater than their own greed.

But look—right there, they are trembling, totally undone with fear. Because God is in the company of the righteous, God is present where love, justice, and fierce authenticity thrive.

These wicked ones, they try to block every path, frustrate the dreams of the poor, the outcast, the ones living on the edge. But they forget—the Lord is our refuge, our safe place, the home that holds us when the world spits us out.

Oh, let salvation come from Zion, from the deep well of holiness! When the Beloved brings us back, when we are restored, let us queer people rejoice and be glad, let all who have been cast aside rise up with joy! We are the ones who've been seen, who will be gathered in love, and we'll sing our truth forever.

Psalm 15

Who, O Lord, can set up camp in your sacred tent? Who can find a home on your holy mountain, that high place where the spirit breathes wild and free?

It's the one who walks with integrity, whose path is woven with righteousness and who speaks the truth straight from their heart, no filters, no masks. They refuse to let their tongue drip with slander, no gossip, no throwing shade. They do no harm to their neighbor, and they don't waste time casting stones at others.

They see right through the bs, through the ones who prey on the weak, and they turn away in disgust. But those who honor the Beloved, those who stand in awe of divine mystery, these they lift up and honor. They keep their word, even (especially) when it costs them, even (especially) when it stings deep. They don't change their mind just to avoid the hard stuff.

They lend a hand to the poor, without expecting anything in return, no interest, no strings attached. And they can't be bought—they won't accept bribes or turn a blind eye when the innocent are thrown under the bus.

The one who lives like this, who walks in love, justice, and fierce compassion—they will never be shaken. They are rooted deep in divine truth, and no storm can knock them down.

Psalm 16

Keep me safe, my God—wrap me in your love, for in you I find refuge from a world that too often seeks to harm us.

I say to you, Holy One, "You are my Beloved, my safe harbor; apart from you, nothing else matters." I look to the queer saints, those who have fought and lived boldly in the land of the living, and I see beauty, resilience, and love shining in them. These are the holy ones in whom I delight—those who live authentically, those who create spaces where we can breathe and just be.

But those who chase after the idols of hate, control, and supremacy—they will find nothing but suffering. I won't follow their ways or give my energy to their violent gods. I will not offer up my spirit to the systems that strip our humanity or utter the names of those who refuse to see us as whole.

You, O Lord, are my portion, my sustenance, my hope. You make my place in the world secure, even when the world sets its sights on us in hatred. Though the bathroom may feel like a battleground, though home may be haunted with threats, though access to health care and basic rights is denied, still, you hold me. The boundary lines you draw around me are safe, and I know I belong.

I will praise you, Lord, for your wisdom guides me in the dark nights when the world feels heavy, and even in those moments, my heart reminds me of your truth. I keep my eyes on you, and with you by my side, I will not be shaken by the fear that grips those around me.

So my heart is glad, my spirit dances in joy, and even my body finds rest, knowing I am held. For you will not abandon me to the realm of the forgotten or leave me to decay in a world of violence and injustice. You reveal the path of life to me—a life where joy is found in your presence, a life that promises pleasures and peace everlasting, at your side.

Psalm 17

My cry is sincere, I'm literally on the bathroom floor in a puddle of
tears.
Listen to my voice as I reach out for justice,
my prayer comes from a place of truth and revolve around my own and
my communities lived experience.

Let my vindication come from you alone;
see the honesty and rightness of my cause.

Even as you search my heart and examine my mind,
you'll find no ill intent within me.
Though many try to sway me,
I've resisted violence and stayed true to a peace-filled path.

I've walked in integrity, holding fast to the path you've shown.
I have not wavered, even when others tried to pull me down.

I call out to you, knowing you will hear me in this flood of emotions...
but dear God, will you hear me?
Show me the depth of your steadfast love,
for you save those who seek refuge from the harm that surrounds them.

Protect me, as one dear to you,
and shield me from the hate that seeks to destroy.
Hide me beneath the shelter of your care
from those who seek to do harm in this world,
from systems of oppression and violence that close in.

Their hearts are hardened by cruelty,
and their words are full of arrogance.
They hunt the vulnerable, waiting for them to stumble,
preying on those who are weak or alone.

But rise up, Lord! Stand against the powers that harm,
bring down those who exploit and deceive.
Deliver us from those who find their reward only in worldly success.

Let those who oppress others bear the weight of their own actions,
and may their own legacy crumble in their hands.

As for me, I will be vindicated by standing in your truth.
When I rise, I will be content with knowing I've lived by your justice,
satisfied by the goodness of your presence.

Psalm 18

I love you, Holy One, wild and unshaken, my safe place when the world calls me by names that are not mine.

You are the ground beneath me when their hate tries to pull me under, the fire in my chest when I have nothing left but my own breath. They tried to drown me in shame, bind me in fear, make me believe I was anything less than divine.

But you—you tore open the sky,
thundered through my bones,
turned the very earth
to make way for me.

You saw me, drenched and breathless, aching to be known. And you pulled me out, not because I was perfect, but because I was yours. You lit a fire in my chest, made my hands steady, taught me to run without falling, to fight without losing myself.

You are the voice in every brave whisper, the pulse in every tender touch, the promise that love has never been a sin.

So I will sing, I will dance, I will be every color of your love—unashamed, unafraid, bathed in the light that no one can steal.

Psalm 19

The sky is screaming poetry, spilling sunrise like a love letter, painting dusk in colors that refuse to be named. The stars don't whisper—they shout, telling a story older than words, a truth too big for any book to hold.

No voice, no language, just the sound of light breaking open the dark. The sun rises like a drag queen taking the stage, bold, radiant, impossible to ignore, strutting across the sky with a heat that holds us all. Your love, O God, is like that—
a brilliance that cannot be tamed,
a warmth that reaches deep,
a truth that refuses to bow to those who would rather keep it quiet.

Your way of love is not a rulebook, but a rhythm, a heartbeat, a path of freedom. It does not bind—it unbinds. It does not shame—it sets free. Sweeter than honey on a lover's lips, stronger than the bones of the earth itself.

So let my words be worthy of this beauty, let my heart stay open to the sky, to the stars, to the story they keep telling—one of love, one of justice, one of a God who delights in every radiant, rebellious, breathtaking thing you made me to be.

PSALM 20

May the Holy One hear you on the days when the world feels like a battle, when the weight of being yourself is met with side-eyes, slurs, silence.

May the name of the Fierce and Tender God be your safe place, your riot shield, your soft landing when the road is rough.

May Love send you help from the ones who know what it is to be cast aside and still rise.

May the wisdom of our queer elders be your sanctuary, their survival your inheritance.
May every dream stitched into your bones be met with a resounding yes —not because you proved yourself worthy, but because you were never anything less.

Some trust in systems, in power, in the ones who sit high and speak low. But we?
We trust in a God
who moves in the margins,
who lifts up the hands of the weary,
who never asks us to shrink.

They will falter—those who build their empires on fear and control— but we will rise, stand tall, sing loud, and take up all the space our souls were made to hold.

O Love, answer us when we call.
O Love, remind us who we are.

Psalm 21

O God of the Glittering and the Gutsy, you delight in us—
not despite who we are, but because of it.

You see the way we walk through fire, the way we turn ashes into altars,
the way we dare to love out loud in a world that calls us too much.

You crown us with garlands of survival, wrap us in robes of resilience.
When we asked for life, you gave us life abundant—not in closets or
cages, but in the full, wild bloom of our becoming.

You have seen our joy, how it refuses to be small.
You have seen our rage, how it burns holy and bright.
You have seen our wounds, how we press gold into the cracks and call it
sacred.

Some wield swords.
Some hoard power.
Some build walls and call it safety.
But we?
We place our trust in the One who bends the arc toward justice, who
laughs in the face of empire, who lifts up the weary and the bold, saying,
You belong. You belong. You belong.

Rise up, O Love.
Rise up in us.

Psalm 22

My God, my God, why does the world speak over me, like my voice was never meant to rise? Why do my prayers climb the air like vines reaching for a sky that refuses to open?

By day, I scream into pulpits that have never held my name with care. By night, I whisper my longing into pillows that remember more tears than dreams. But still—no answer, no rest, just the echo of a silence I do not deserve.

And yet—I know you.
I have seen you in the breath of the bound, in the voices of the banned, in the bodies of those who will never fold themselves small enough to fit inside a closet again. Our ancestors called on you—the ones who ran, who hid, who prayed, who rewrote their own names to keep their stories alive. You held them, you heard them, you were the fire inside their ribs when the world called them unnatural.

But me?
I am a thread unraveling. I am a name mispronounced on the tongues of those who do not care to learn it. They laugh, they scorn, they say, "Where is your God now?" as if holiness could only live in bodies that look like theirs. But you have been with me since the first time I loved without apology, since the first time I saw my reflection and did not turn away. Do not stay far from me now. Danger is close, and I am tired of running. I am poured out, empty from years of fighting to be something the world would rather erase. They cut pieces from my story, pick apart my pronouns like bones, call me lost as if I have not found myself a thousand times already.

But you, Holy One—you are not like them.
You hear me.
You see me.
You are the voice that calls me whole when the world calls me broken.

Come quickly—rescue me from the hands of those who only know love as a weapon. Let me rise again in the sanctuary of the unseen, let me speak my name in the streets of the silenced, let me dance in the riot of the unashamed.

The poor will eat and be satisfied. The trans kid will rest without fear. The drag queen will sing without shame. The nonbinary elder will be honored as wisdom. The ones who love in ways the world calls strange will know they are your delight.

And the generations to come—the ones still waiting for a world that does not ask them to be less than holy—they will hear the story of a God who has always, always, called them good.

Psalm 23

The Holy is my shepherd—not the church with locked doors, not the
voices that say *love has rules*, not the hands that hold scripture like a
blade.
No—the Holy is my shepherd, and I have everything I need. They lead
me to quiet places, where my name is safe in every mouth, where my
love is not a debate, where my body is not a battleground. They lay me
down in meadows wide enough for all the ways I have ever belonged.
They restore the parts of me the world tried to erase.

They walk me through valleys where laws have turned my existence into
a crime, where some call me abomination while claiming to speak for
God. But I will not be afraid—
not with the Holy by my side, not with their staff pulling me close, not
with their whisper reminding me I was never a mistake.

They set a table before me, wide as liberation,
sturdy as stone rolled away. And look—every seat is filled with the ones
they told me wouldn't make it. The trans saints, the queer prophets, the
lovers who held hands in the dark, the ancestors who hid, who ran, who
prayed to be something other than holy.

You anoint my head with oil,
call me chosen,
call me beloved,
call me yours.
My cup overflows—not with shame, not with fear, but with the joy of
knowing
I was always meant to be here.

Goodness and mercy chase after me, like a freedom song still being
written.
And I will dwell in the house of the Holy—not just someday, not just
when I fit their mold, but right here, right now, for as long as love is love.

Psalm 24

The earth is the Holy's, and everything in it—every river that sings free-dom, every mountain carved with resilience, every body, every heartbeat, every love too wild to be tamed.

The Holy built this world on justice, set the foundation with grace, opened the sky so light could touch even those who were told they belonged in the shadows.

Who gets to stand in sacred places?
Who gets to climb the hill of belonging?
Not just the ones who fit the mold, not just the ones who learned to blend in—but the ones with open hands, the ones who love without agenda, the ones who do not weaponize faith to build walls higher than hope.

Lift up your heads, O gates! Swing wide, ancient doors! Make room for the Holy One—not a king in robes of power, but a shepherd of the outcast, a healer of the wounded, a savior whose hands have only ever held love.

Who is this Holy One?
The One who fights for the forgotten, the One who dances at pride parades, the One who sits beside the abandoned and calls them beloved.

Lift up your heads, O gates! Swing wide, ancient doors!
For the Holy is coming in—and they are bringing all of us home.

Psalm 25

Please, dear God,
don't let me get tangled in the trap of shame,
don't let the voices of hate turn down the volume on my truth.
Shame's got no claim here, no weight
against the heartbeat I've anchored in you—
you, the pulse of my hope, the ground I stand on.

Lead me into the way of your expansive love,
show me what it means to walk boldly toward justice,
to live in what's real and raw and true.
And help me remember to return to you to be renewed in hope,
every day.

Remind me (often) of the mercy you carry like breath,
the love that was here before time was spoken into being.
Remind me so that I have the ability to forget the wreckage I've dragged,
the fumbles and the heavy baggage.
Remind me so that I have full understanding that you see me through
that lens of love,
because you, God, you're just that good.

You are so good, Holy Spirit of Hope,
and even when I'm lost or stumbling,
you're there, whispering the way back.
You're the one leading all who open their hearts,
teaching us the art of kindness, the beauty of grace.

Every path you walk beside us is stitched with love, laced with truth,
for all of us who want to live into this world you dreamed,
this world you've set in motion.

Psalm 26

Judge me, O Love, but let it be by the truth of who I am—not by the fears of those who refuse to see me whole. I have walked in integrity, not the kind that fits in pews too small for my spirit, but the kind that stands tall even when the world says, shrink.

I have trusted you, held tight to your love when others let go, when doors slammed,
when voices whispered, not enough, not enough, not enough.
But I am here—still standing, still sacred, still singing your name with every breath of my becoming.

Search me, O God, see the way my heart beats steady with the rhythm of truth. I will not sit with those who sharpen their tongues into knives, who twist love into law and call it righteousness. I refuse to dim my light for a table that was never set for me.

But oh, the places you lead me—where laughter echoes holy, where hands hold hands without fear or shame, where justice and joy kiss in the streets and call it worship.

So here I stand, in the wide-open sanctuary of your love, feet firm, voice loud, singing, Hallelujah, I am still here.

Psalm 27

The Holy is my light—my fire, my heartbeat, the glow that refuses to be snuffed out. Whom shall I fear? The Divine is my safe place, the home I carry in my bones, even when the world tries to evict me.

When hatred marches toward me, with doctrines like daggers, when they call me lost, call me wrong, call me anything but beloved—they will stumble on their own words.
Love will not be undone.

Even if the whole world turns against me, if family names me stranger, if the church pews grow cold at my presence, I will not be afraid. I have learned this love is bigger than buildings, wider than any gatekeepers' arms.

One thing I ask, one thing I long for: to dwell in the house of Love all the days of my life, not just in whispered prayers, but in every wide-open space where laughter and justice dance together, where queer hands hold one another without fear of who is watching.

For in the day of trouble, Love hides me in Her embrace, pulls me close under wings that have always made room. She sets me high upon the truth of my own sacred worth,
and I will not bow to shame.

So I will sing, sing with a voice that will not quiet, sing like someone who knows they were never a mistake, who was formed, named, and called **very good** before the world tried to rewrite the story.

Listen to me, Love—I am calling out, not just for myself, but for every child who has been told they are too much, or not enough, or unworthy of the altar. Do not hide your face from us.

Even if mother and father let go, even if home is something I have to build with my own bare hands, I know you will take me in. You will be the family, the place, the belonging.

Teach me your ways, O Love. Show me the roads where justice walks, where courage takes up space, where liberation sings our names.

I believe this:
I will see the goodness of God in this life, not just the next. Not just in Heaven, but here, in bodies unashamed, in love without fear, in a world where all are free.

So I will wait on the Holy—not in silence, but in hope, with fists uncurled, with a heart wide open, with a love that will not be moved.

Psalm 28

O Love, I call to you—not in whispers, but in bold, unashamed cries, in the voices of those told they don't belong, of hands reaching for a love that has always been theirs to hold.

Be my rock, my steady ground, when the world calls me sin, when they twist your name into a weapon and call it righteousness. If you stay silent, if you don't show up,
they will say you were never here. But I have seen you—in the arms that pull me close, in the voices that rise for justice, in the defiant joy of being exactly who you made me to be.

Do not let me fall into the hands of those who preach love but practice exclusion, who say "Come as you are" but mean "Only if you change." Their prayers are empty echoes, their kindness a locked door.

But Love—you are not like them. You do not erase. You do not demand silence. You do not ask me to be less so that others can be comfortable.

So I lift my hands to you, to the sanctuary not built by shame, but by every whispered "You are enough," by every rainbow flag waving in the storm, by every love that dares to exist when the world says it shouldn't.

Blessed be the One who does not flinch at our truth, who does not turn away from the ones the world has called lost.

You are my strength, my shield, the one who holds me up when the weight of their words
tries to pull me under.

I trust you—
not because I was told to,
but because I have found you
in every moment of love
that was real and free and true.

Love is love,
and you are love.
And I will not be moved.

Psalm 29

Give honor to the One who speaks our names before the world ever
dared to—
who etched our truth into the marrow of our bones,
who saw us whole when others saw only questions.

Give honor to the One whose voice is thunder, shaking the roots of a
world that tries to make us whisper. The voice of God is not silent—it
cracks like lightning, carves rivers through stone, turns brittle laws into
dust. It roars through the wild woods, calls dead names to fall like
autumn leaves, and makes way for the names we have always known
in the deepest parts of ourselves.

The voice of God splits the skies wide open—a baptism of rain for every
trans body told they could not be holy. God's voice is a flood, washing
away the fear, drowning out the shame, leaving only the truth:
You are mine.
You are whole.
You are beloved.

And in their temple—not one built by hands, but by every brave breath
we take, by every step toward living free—we cry out with the storm:

Glory to the God
of the loud and the unshaken,
of the queer and the unbroken,
of the trans and the thriving.

Love reigns.
Justice reigns.
And peace—real peace—
is coming like a wave.

Psalm 30

I lift my voice to you, Holy One, for you have seen me—whole, not missing, not lacking, not waiting to be completed. You have pulled me from the pit of expectation, where love was only counted in romance, where wholeness was measured in pairs.

I cried out, and you heard me—not as lonely, not as lost, but as someone whose heart beats to a different rhythm, whose joy is not wrapped in longing, whose love is as vast as the sky but never needs to be tethered.

They told me love was one road, that joy had only one shape, but you, God of infinite ways, showed me a path unmarked, a road wide enough for me to dance alone, to dance with friends, to dance with the whole aching world without needing one hand to hold.

Your anger, they say, is but a moment—but oh, how long did I sit in the sorrow of a world that did not understand me? How many nights did I grieve a loneliness that was never mine to carry? But morning has come, and the weeping has turned to dancing, not in anyone's arms, but in the vastness of my own enoughness.

You have turned the lie of my incompleteness into dust.
You have clothed me in joy.
You have unfastened the weight of "almost" and "not yet"
and given me a song of already, of always, of whole.

So I will not be silent.
I will not let the world tell my story for me.
I will sing to you, God of the Unbound,
for I am enough—
I have always been enough—
and my love, just as it is,
will never run dry.

Psalm 31

In you, Holy One, I find my refuge—not in closets, not in silence, not in bending myself to fit a world too small for my spirit. Hold me, not to make me smaller, but to remind me I was never meant to be less.

They told me to hide, to soften my voice, to straighten my wrists, to wear a love that didn't fit like a hand-me-down lie. But you, God of the Bold and Unbowed, have always known me as whole.

Turn your ear to me, not because I am weak, but because I am weary of proving my worth
to those who build their faith on fear. Be my rock, not to cage me in, but to be the mountain I stand upon when the world tries to wash me away.

They set traps—whispers in the pews, policies that call themselves love but taste like erasure, family that speaks in past tense when they say my name. But you see me as I am, and in your hands, I am safe.

I hear the echoes of their shame, the twisting of scripture into shackles, the way they say "love" and mean "leave yourself behind." But my love, my truth, my queerness—these are not burdens; these are holy, these are bright, these are divine.

You see my tears, but you also see my joy.
You hold my grief, but you also hold my pride.
You do not ask me to change,
only to breathe deep,
to step forward,
to live.

So I will not let shame swallow me.
I will not let fear steal my song.
I will stand in the wide, open light of your love,
queer and unshakeable,
and I will sing.

Psalm 32

Blessed are the ones who refuse to apologize for existing, whose love needs no confession, whose truth is not a secret to be swallowed whole. Blessed are the ones who walk unburdened, who know shame was never theirs to carry.

For too long, I held my breath, kept my voice small, let silence sit heavy on my chest. I thought if I made myself invisible, I'd be safe. But hiding is just another kind of dying,
and I was made for more than survival.

Then I cracked open, spilled every truth I had locked inside, and you, Holy One, you met me there—not with judgment, not with fear, but with open arms and a whisper:
You were never a mistake.

Now, when the storms come, when the hate rolls in like a tide, I don't drown—I rise.
Because you are my safe place, not in a way that cages me, but in a way that says, run free.

So listen up, world:
queer love is holy.
Trans bodies are divine.
Asexual hearts beat with the rhythm of the sacred.
Nonbinary souls reflect the infinite expanse of the Divine.

You, who would shame us—you will not win.
Love is louder.
Truth is brighter.
And joy?
Joy is a revolution you can't erase.

So I will dance in the streets, laugh with my whole chest, live so boldly that even the stars take notes—because this life, this love, this body, this breath, all of it is blessed.

Psalm 33

Sing out, loud and unashamed—not just with your voice, but with the way you exist, with the way you take up space like you were never meant to be anything but a masterpiece.

Praise belongs in the hands of the ones who dared to survive, who refused to be erased, who love like a protest and dance like a prayer.

The Holy One paints galaxies with their breath, stitches oceans into being with their fingertips, and still—still, they made you exactly as you are, no edits, no regrets, no footnotes explaining you away.

The whole earth hums with their presence—in the laughter of queer elders who tell stories of a love too strong to be buried, in the courage of trans youth who walk through fire just to be seen, in the quiet breath of the ones who are still learning that they, too, are sacred.

The Divine sees through the smoke and mirrors, sees beyond the laws written to erase us, the pulpits turned into battlegrounds, the prayers twisted into weapons. Powerful hands build empires—but the Holy One builds revolutions.

Look—the world is shifting, the old ways are cracking. No government, no doctrine, no fear-drenched theology can stand against the force of love rising up like a tidal wave.

So we will not hush our joy.
We will not shrink our light.
We will live,
we will love,
we will be,
until the whole world sings along.

Psalm 34

No matter what happens, I'll keep speaking truth. I've been through some stuff, and God is still the one I praise. Let those who've been crushed by life hear this and find some hope. Come on, let's shout it together—let's lift up God's name, loud and proud.

I called out to God when I was wrecked, and God showed up. Every fear that had me by the throat—God broke those chains. The ones who look to God, you can see it in their faces—they're glowing with life, no longer carrying the weight of shame. I've been down and out, calling to God from my pit, and God heard me. Rescued me from all the hell I was going through.

God's spirit camps around those who dare to keep going, who stand up even when the world tries to beat them down. And God protects them. Taste this for yourself—just see how good God is. Those who take refuge in the Divine find a kind of blessing that can't be measured. Listen up, you who are exhausted and oppressed—those who stand in awe of God, they're never left stranded. The strong and privileged might find themselves empty and starving, but those who seek God's justice never lack for anything that truly matters.

Gather round, children of the struggle, and I'll tell you how to live in the reverence of the Holy One. You want a life that means something? You want days that feel like more than just survival? Then watch your mouth. Don't let your words be weapons. Keep your lips from spreading poison. Turn away from the crap that destroys you and do good instead. Chase after peace—like, chase it down relentlessly, even when the world makes it hard to find.

God's eyes are on those who fight the good fight, and God's ears are tuned into their cries. But the systems of evil that keep people down? God's got no patience for that. Those who oppress, they don't last.

When the broken cry out, God listens. God pulls them out of the pit, piece by piece. God is near to those whose hearts have been shattered, and lifts up those whose spirits have been crushed under the weight of it all. Yeah, the ones who walk the path of justice, they've got their share of battles, but God's with them in every single one. God's protection runs deep—it holds their very bones together, even when everything else is falling apart.

Evil? It devours itself. The wicked end up victims of their own violence. But God? God saves those who serve, who keep showing up, who keep seeking justice. Not one person who takes refuge in God is ever left without hope or without help.

Psalm 35

Holy One, they come for us with sharpened tongues, with laws like shackles, with pulpits turned into war rooms. They twist your name into a weapon and hurl it at our joy—but we are still here.

Rise up, Love that will not be silenced, be the shield between us and their hate, the fire that burns through their fear. Call out every lie spoken in your name, every hand that has ever raised scripture like a blade against our bodies.

They stalk us in the streets, in the pews, in the courtroom, in our own families' eyes.
They spit out prayers like poison, prayers that smell like erasure, like closets, like graves.

But you, O God of holy resistance, have always walked beside the outcast. You carve spaces where we can breathe, where we can dance, where we can love without apology.

Let their whispers unravel.
Let the weight of their judgment collapse.
Let the truth ring out louder than every sermon meant to break us.

For we will not break.
We will not bow.
We will not be anything less than the dazzling, divine creation you shaped us to be.

So we will rejoice, not in their downfall—but in our survival. In every hand held, every kiss stolen beneath streetlights, every chosen family built from the rubble.

And when they ask how we endure, how we keep singing, keep loving, keep rising—
we will tell them: Because Love has always been on our side.

Psalm 36

They talk like they own holiness, like love is a gated community and we're just trespassing. They build walls out of scriptures they don't even understand, stacking verses like bricks, like checkpoints, like "You don't belong here."

But oh, if they only knew. If they only knew the way your love moves— not like a doctrine, but like a flood. Like a pulse. Like a protest song spilling from a hundred throats in the streets at midnight.

Your love, God, it doesn't tiptoe, doesn't check IDs at the door. It roars like oceans swallowing shorelines, like ballroom queens spinning under flashing lights, like first kisses when no one's watching.

The ones who deal in fear don't know real power. They mistake control for divinity, mistake shame for righteousness, mistake themselves for you.

But you— you are the arms flung open wide, the neon sign buzzing "All Are Welcome," the quiet whisper saying, "You don't have to hide anymore."

So we step into your mercy, feet bare, hearts unarmored. We drink deep from your well, unafraid. And when they ask how we dare to call ourselves beloved, we will say:

Because Love has always been louder than their fear.

Psalm 37

Don't waste your breath on those who spit fire at your joy, who lace
their prayers with poison and call it love. Their power is paper-thin,
their empires built on sand, and you—you are the ocean, you are the
storm.

Trust in the Divine that made you exactly as you are. Plant your roots
deep in that truth. Dance in the streets like the whole sky is watching.
Let your existence be praise, your laughter be worship, your love be
revolution.

Let them grumble.
Let them twist scripture like barbed wire.
Their hate won't last.
Their voices will fade
like a sermon no one remembers.
But you—
you are an echo of something eternal,
something holy,
something too bright to be dimmed.

Rest in that. Breathe in that. Hold fast to the promise that you are here
for a reason, that you belong, that no one—
not your parents,
not the church,
not the law—
can take away the love the Divine has woven into your bones.

And when the world is cruel, when justice feels like a dream we'll never
wake into, don't give up.
Keep loving.
Keep fighting.
Keep walking toward the light like you already know the whole
kingdom is waiting for you
with open arms.

Psalm 38

Some days, my body feels like a battle—every breath, a casualty. I carry wounds the world refuses to see, scars etched with whispers of "too much" and "not enough" in the same breath. Shame hangs heavy on my shoulders, a weight I was never meant to bear.

God, I am tired.
Tired of running,
tired of bending myself
into something more palatable,
tired of pretending the silence doesn't hurt.

The world calls me a mistake, but I know—I know you do not craft errors.
You are the Artist, and I am not an accident of your hands.

Still, the loneliness swallows me whole some nights. Still, I hear the laughter of those who have never had to carve space for themselves. Still, I feel the sting of words sharpened into weapons by those who claim to speak for you.

But I know—I know you are near, closer than my next inhale. You sit with me in the ache, in the longing, in the messy, holy truth of my existence. You are the pulse in my chest, the whisper in my bones: "You are mine. You are loved."

So I will keep rising, even when the weight tries to pull me under.
I will keep hoping,
even when hope feels like a stranger.
I will keep loving,
because love—
true, boundless, fierce love—
has always been your way.

Psalm 39

I tried to bite my tongue, to shrink myself into the quiet, to play respectability like a lifeline, but the silence burned. It sat heavy in my chest, begging to be screamed into existence.

I thought if I just behaved, if I softened my edges, if I smiled and stayed small, the world would leave me be. But respectability won't save me, and silence was never my calling.

God, you see me—
not just the me they want, but the whole damn radiant, messy, expansive, queer constellation of me. And I know—deep in my soul, I know —I was not made to be a shadow.

So why do I still feel like a ghost haunting my own life? Why does the world still act like I'm a phase, a problem, a glitch in the system? I watch the same cycles spin: hatred masquerading as holiness, fear disguised as tradition, and I wonder—how long, O God?

don't want my days spent in whispered apologies for who I am. I don't want my breath wasted on battles that should never have been fought. I want to live—fully, loudly, unapologetically free.

So I open my mouth, and out comes fire.
Out comes love so wild it cannot be tamed.
Out comes a voice that will not be silenced.
Because you, O God, never asked me to be small.

Psalm 40

I waited.
God, you know I waited—in the in-between, in the almosts, in the
maybe-one-days that stretched into never.
I waited while the world told me to change, to hush, to bend myself into
something easier to love.

But you, O God—
you never asked me to break myself down for their comfort. You pulled
me up from the pit of second-guessing, of late-night prayers for a
different body, a different heart, a love that wouldn't make me a question mark in my own family.

You set my feet on solid ground, but not the kind that cages me in—
no, you gave me ground that lets me dance.
And so I do.
I move, I shimmer, I take up space.
I sing a new song, one I wrote
for the ones still waiting,
for the ones told their love is too much,
their voice too loud,
their truth too messy for Sunday morning.

But you, O Holy One, are not a God of closets and cages. You are the
God of coming out, of stepping into light, of turning shame into something holy.

So I will not be quiet. I will tell the story—our story—the one written
in every queer breath, every hand held without fear, every name
reclaimed, every pronoun spoken like a blessing.

Great is your love, O God,
and I will not keep it to myself.

Psalm 41

Blessed are the ones who show up with snacks and softness, who sit bedside when the world feels like too much, who Venmo ten bucks with the note "for your joy, babe."
Blessed are the caregivers, the chosen family, the ones who say, "you're not a burden, you're a miracle still unfolding."

God sees the ones who stay soft in a world that sharpens its edges—sees you holding someone's hand through their fever dreams, their grief spirals, their gender euphoria when the mirror finally smiles back.

When we feel like walking disasters, like we've cried too much or loved too loudly, God is the one who says, "Rest here. I've got you."
God nurses our broken hearts like they're sacred things—because they are. Because we are.

eople talk. They say things they don't understand. They make jokes that cut, sling words "sin" and "choice" like they've never known what it's like to be holy and hunted at the same time.

Even those we trusted—they ghost us, talk over us, forget our pronouns, forget our names.

But you, Love that will not let go, are still here, whispering:
"You are enough.
You are mine.
You are queerly, wonderfully made."

You lift us up, call us beloved when the world calls us broken.

So we rise—with glitter in our veins and protest in our pulse, singing praise to the One who keeps showing up exactly when we think we're too much to hold.

Blessed be the God of rainbow promises and wild, relentless grace. From everlasting to everlasting, love is love is love and it never ends.

BOOK II

PSALMS 42-72

Psalm 42

My soul is thirsty, like I've danced too hard at Pride and haven't had water in days—I'm parched for presence, for peace that doesn't question my pronouns or my right to be. I long for Love like a deer pants for cool rivers, like I'm searching for a mirror that sees me the way I was always meant to be seen.

Where is your God now? They ask with smirks at family dinners, in church pews that feel more like prisons. And I, I don't have the answers —just the ache
of being whole in a world that calls wholeness a problem to fix.

I remember the joy parades, marching with arms linked, glitter and sweat and songs that make the sky weep. We were loud, and holy, and seen. But now?
Now, the silence hums in my bones, and my heart feels heavy with all the laws that say I shouldn't exist.

Why are you cast down, O my soul? Why this weight in your chest like a closet door that never fully opened? Hope, I whisper, like it's a spell I'm still learning to cast.
Hope in the Love that made you—exactly you—and called you good.

The waves keep coming. I drown in headlines, in hashtags for those who didn't make it,
in vigils for names that should've had more birthdays.

Still, deep calls to deep—and somewhere beneath the noise, the drag shows, the protests, the love letters to ourselves, I hear it—the pulse of the Divine beating in rhythm with my own.

By day, there's rage and resilience.
By night, a song—soft and sure, a lullaby for the broken-hearted.

I ask, Are you still with me, Love? And I swear, in the wind that lifts my flag, in the stranger who calls me "they" without hesitation, I hear:
Always.

So why are you cast down, O my soul?
Rise.
Let hope be the tattoo on your wrist,
the anthem in your lungs.
For you will praise again—
not in spite of your queerness,
but because of it.

Psalm 43

Stand with me, Love, defend my right to be—to breathe in this body and not apologize for existing. Deliver me from systems that misgender and mouths that spew hate in holy tones.

Why does justice feel like it's on vacation when I need it most? Why do rainbow flags get burned while pulpits stay silent?

You are my safe place, my chosen family when blood turns bitter. So why do I feel like I'm shouting into an empty sky, asking why and hearing only echoes?

Send out your truth like protest chants that shake the streets, send your light like a trans kid's first name spoken with pride. Let them lead me to sacred spaces that don't ask me to change before entering.

There, in the heart of Love, I'll dance. Not just survive—but live,
thrive,
be whole.

I'll bring my song, an offering of joy from a soul once caged but now fiercely free.

Why are you downcast, my beautiful, queer soul? Why the ache? Hope still lives in every march, every pronoun respected, every hand held tight in love.

We will rise—
singing,
shining,
untamed.
Love is not done.

Psalm 44

We've heard the stories—
the ones our queer elders whispered in closets, in back alleys, in sanctuaries not built for them. They told us how Love moved, how hands held
trembling hands and made a kind of holy out of survival.

You, Divine One, fought for them, pulled them through the fires of
hate, through laws that erased them, through families that turned
"unconditional" into a joke they never laughed at.

It wasn't with swords or fists or votes, but with hearts beating loud
enough to crack the sky
and prayers stitched from the threads of rainbow flags that refused to
fall.

We trust in that same Love. Not the kind that demands we shrink, but
the kind that says:
you are enough
in all your gender-bending,
boundary-breaking,
beautiful becoming.

Still—we feel abandoned. We show up, love loud, and yet the world still
calls us "too much" or not enough. Still, we're hunted by laws, by
preachers with poisoned tongues, by silence that screams louder than
hate ever could.

We're not backing down. Even if you feel far, even if the nights get long,
we'll keep dancing in defiance. Because we haven't forgotten you—
we've just been bruised and bent by a world that fears what it cannot
name.

Wake up, Beloved. Do you see the drag queens being banned? The
youth sleeping on streets because "coming out" meant losing everything?
Our tears water this soil—don't let them be wasted.

We know you're Love. Fierce. Forever. So show up for us the way we've shown up for each other. Not because we earned it—but because Love always does.

We're still here. We've still got glitter on our faces and grit in our souls. Rise for us, with us. Let this be the story they tell: how the queers loved and were never left alone.

Psalm 45

My heart overflows with words too sacred for silence, a love song blooming from lips that once trembled with fear. I write these lines for every queer soul who has ever dared to love in the face of erasure.

You—radiant in your truth, bold in your becoming—are clothed not in robes of conformity, but in authenticity stitched by your own hands. Your beauty is not defined by their gaze; it is fierce, divine, like a flame that refuses to go out.

Your words bring justice with softness and steel. You do not conquer with swords, but with truth and tenderness. You are the embodiment of love that does not apologize.

The Divine anoints you not for who the world demands you be, but for who you are: nonbinary royalty, transcendent and tender, bending gender and expectation into something holy.

You walk among us, queer kin, chosen family, lifting our chins, reminding us we are worthy—not despite our queerness, but because of it.

Your love is not a rebellion; it is a revolution of joy. You kiss without shame, hold hands without fear, write your name in the sky of the sacred.

Your life is a testament—to survival, to resilience, to the holy riot that is queer love unfurling like a rainbow after centuries of storms.

We honor you, celebrate you, lift you up like a banner for all who thought they had to hide.
You are the psalm we never thought we'd live to sing—but here we are. And we will not be silent.

Love reigns, and it wears all colors.

Let this be the anthem that echoes across generations:
queer love is sacred,

our bodies are temples,
our stories—holy scripture.
And the Divine delights in us.

Forever.
And always.
Amen.

Psalm 46

Our God is a safe house, a sanctuary with rainbow walls and doors wide open—no passwords, no gatekeepers, just a fierce welcome and a love that refuses to flinch.

When the world shakes, when the headlines scream that we're too much or not enough—we do not run, we do not shrink. We stand rooted, chest out, heels (or boots) planted, because Love is our refuge and we— we are unshakable.

Let the systems crack, let patriarchy crumble, let the mountains of oppression slide into the sea. We will dance on the shifting ground, knowing the Divine is in our midst—a Presence that doesn't ask us to change, to conform, to dim.

There is a river that runs through our souls—clear, bold, flowing with the joy of chosen family, queer laughter at midnight, and tears shed in safety.

The Holy One is with us—not just in pews, but in pride parades, drag shows, coffee shop corners, gender-affirming clinics, and whispered "I love yous" at dawn.

God is in the soft, the flamboyant, the fierce, the fluid. They break the bow, snap the sword, and smash every weapon of shame, every lie that told us we were unworthy.

"Be still," They say, "and know I am here—in your transness, your queerness, your ace identity, your nonbinary beauty. I am here—and I am not leaving."

The Divine, our Rock, our Fire, our Fierce Protector, is with us—and in Them, we are enough. We are powerful. We are whole.

Forever
and always.

Psalm 47

Clap your hands, all you fierce beings, snap your fingers, stomp your boots—let joy erupt from the floorboards of every drag bar, sanctuary, kitchen table.

Shout to Love with the voice that's been silenced too long.
Lift it up, belt it out like your favorite song at the queer karaoke night where everyone is family and no one needs permission to shine.

Because our God—not some old man in the sky with a list of rules—but the God of glitter, grace, and grit, is wrapped in majesty, clothed in the fabrics of our gender euphoria, our trans pride flags, our softest selves and boldest truths.

Love reigns—not with fear, not with domination, but with the power of chosen family,
of showing up, of holding hands in the dark and whispering,
"You are sacred."

They have ascended on the rhythm of our laughter, on the chorus of protest chants, on the hush of prayer that doesn't need words.

Sing praises—not to kings or queens of empires, but to the Sovereign of the exiles, the runaways, the radiant souls who build altars out of resistance and praise out of survival.

Our God gathers us—
the misfits,
the marvels,
the ones who were told to sit down but chose to dance instead.

They are enthroned, not in cathedrals of gold, but in our hearts, our hugs, our sacred, messy lives.

So, rise up, all you beloved queers, wave your flags, light your candles, kiss your lovers, and know:
Love reigns.
And we?
We are the proof.

Psalm 48

Great is Love—not the cheap kind sold in Hallmark cards, but the kind we make when we stitch our broken pieces together and say, "Here. This is holy."

Love's presence pulses in the heart of every queer sanctuary, every glitter-streaked pride parade, every living room altar where chosen family gathers to tell stories and be seen.

Beautiful is this city we build—not walled in stone, but bound by trust, by radical welcome, by the music of laughter and the rhythm of healing.

We have known oppression—seen the powers that be quake in fear of our brilliance, our softness, our refusal to disappear.

They've tried to erase us, to exile us, but their fortress walls crumble in the face of our truth.

For Love is our compass, our map, our lighthouse when the night feels endless.

Walk the streets of this sacred place—feel the safety, the joy, the fierce resilience etched into every mural, every dance floor, every protest line.

This is the story we tell to the next generation:
that Love is here,
now,
and always.

Not just a fleeting feeling, but a dwelling place, a refuge, a home for every queer soul who ever thought they didn't belong.

Because here's the truth—we belong. We have always belonged.

And Love?
Love never fails
to remind us of that.

PSALM 49

Listen up—
this is for the dreamers, the boundary-breakers, the ones who've been
told "you're too much" or "not enough" in a world obsessed with labels
and ladders.

Everyone—queer, trans, ace, bi, drag queen, leather dyke, non-binary
nebula wrapped in flesh—hear this truth.

Money talks,

It buys megaphones and builds empires that try to drown out our
voices, but it can't buy forever. The rich, the famous, those clinging to
power with bloodied fists—they die just like the rest of us. No amount
of gold can bribe the grave.

But love—
real, raw, chosen family kind of love—
lives on.

Their wealth fades; our truth echoes in protest chants, in wedding vows
said under open skies, in the pulse of a nightclub where we dance like we
are free because we are.

Don't envy their palaces; they're built on sand, on silence, on the bones
of those they buried to reach the top.

We, we build with glitter and grit, with memory and defiance.
Our legacy isn't hoarded—
it's lived,
shared,
carried in every act of kindness we give without permission.

When death comes, we won't be owned, won't be erased—because our
stories won't die with us.

They are stitched into the fabric of eternity, into every sacred breath that
says, "I exist. I belong. I am beloved."

So don't be afraid. Don't be fooled. Don't be silenced. Our worth is not measured in dollars or followers, but in the light we dare to shine into every shadow.

Love is our currency. Truth is our inheritance. And in the end?
We rise.
We always rise.

Psalm 50

The Holy calls—
not from gilded altars or megachurch pulpits with fog machines and
choreographed praise, but from the city streets at dawn, from the drag
brunch where laughter is holy, from the protest where love walks with a
clenched fist and glitter is a weapon against despair.

From sunrise to moonrise, the Divine is speaking through the beat of
our hearts, through the shimmer of skin that defies gender norms,
through every breath that says "I exist" in a world that tried to write us
out of the story.

God doesn't need your burnt offerings, your fake apologies, your token
diversity panels.
What She wants?
Your honesty.
Your justice.
Your queer truth that refuses to conform, your love unbartered and
unashamed.

You think your rituals impress? You think She didn't see you turning
away the trans woman at the communion table? Didn't hear the slurs
wrapped in theology you claimed was "love"? Let's get this straight—
the Divine is not your puppet, not a brand to be marketed or a rulebook
to weaponize.

She's a fierce nonbinary force of cosmic compassion, not impressed by
your churches full of gold, but by the courage of the closeted kid who
dares to come out even when it means losing everything.

To those who walk with love burning like a neon sign in their chest—
who speak truth even when their voices shake, who open their doors to
the exiled, the displaced, the ones told "you don't belong"—
She is with you.

She is you. They are Them.
Divine beyond binaries, beyond borders, beyond the boxes we've been
forced into.

This is the call:
not to sacrifice, but to solidarity.
Not to empty songs, but to sacred defiance.

So gather, beloveds. Paint your faces like warpaint. Hold hands like a revolution. Lift your voices, not in fear, but in fierce, fearless worship. And know:
Love is watching. Truth is rising. And justice, queer and wild, is on Her way.

Psalm 51

Have mercy on me, O Love that holds all of who I am.
Not just the parts they call acceptable, but the softness, the fire, the too-much-ness they tried to strip away.
See me in the fullness of my becoming—
in the scars and the survival, in the beauty they said was broken.

Wash away the shame they taught me to wear like a second skin.
Scrub off the whispers, the slurs,
the hands that pushed me out of pews
and the doctrines that tried to make me disappear.
I have carried their words too long,
pressed them into my ribs until I thought they were mine.

But you—
you have always seen me whole.
Before they told me my body was wrong,
before they wrote rules to keep me from love,
you knit me together with colors they refused to name.
You called me radiant before they called me sinner.

Create in me a heart that beats in the rhythm of truth.
Breathe into these tired bones a spirit that cannot be erased.
Let me sing the song of the outcast made holy,
of the exile called beloved,
of the one they tried to bury,
rising, rising, rising—

not in spite of who I am,
but because of it

Psalm 52

Fools say in their hearts, "There is no Love here." They build walls out of fear and call it safety. They turn away from mercy, bury kindness six feet under and still wonder why the earth shakes beneath them.

Their gods wear suits, speak in binary tongues, sit on thrones made of exclusion. But we know better—
we've danced in the rain of rejected prayers, and still, our joy rose like sunflowers from cracked concrete.

They call us corrupt, say we're ruining the world with rainbow flags and chosen names, but their mirrors don't show the harm etched into their own hands.

Not one of them understands—not the grief behind our glitter, not the strength in our softness, not the sacred in our resistance.

Love looked down, searched the streets for someone—anyone—who still believed in justice that doesn't pick sides, in faith without chains, in bodies unpoliced by doctrine.

And Love found us—
the queer kids with broken hearts stitched together with hope, the elders who survived silence, the dreamers who dared to imagine a world where everyone could breathe.

We are not the fools. We are the truth-tellers, the joy-makers, the holy rebels.

And when the Divine rises—not in wrath but in wild, wondrous love—
we will be ready, arms open wide, hearts like battle drums, singing:
Love is real.
Love is here.
Love is us.

Psalm 53

They say we are a phase, a trend, a glitch in the system. Call us lost, as if they've ever dared to look for us.

The fool says in their heart, "There is no need to change." No need for justice, no need for truth that cracks the pavement we've all been told to walk.

They scroll past suffering like it's background noise—while their hands build walls, their words erase names, their laws shrink lives.

From the heavens, Love sees it all—sees hearts chained to ego, to empire, to the illusion of "normal."

And still, She searches: for the brave, the bold, the kind-hearted misfits who refuse to let cruelty be the last word.

But there's so much pretending—performances masked as faith, as morality, as tradition.
The systems devour the vulnerable, and call it order.

One day—and may it come soon—the lie will shatter. And those who clung to power like a god, will see how empty their fists really were.

We, the ones they exiled, mocked, forgot—will rise, not in vengeance, but in the joy of knowing we survived every "no," every silence.

Salvation won't come with a sword. It will come with a dance, with open arms, with the laughter of queer youth who never gave up.

Let the fools speak.
Let them scoff.
Love is watching,
and we are still here—
holy,
unshaken,
free.

Psalm 54

Save me, not because I'm perfect—but because I'm real.

Because I've bled truth onto sidewalks that never saw me, into systems that never held me.
Save me, because your name is stitched into every part of me they said didn't belong.

Listen.
Can you hear it?
Their words sharp as shattered glass, their eyes heavy with judgment—they don't see my heart, only the version of me they were taught to fear.

They say I'm a threat to their comfort, to their categories. But I'm just breathing, loving, living outside the lines they drew like fences to keep joy from spilling over.

They rise against me—not with swords, but with silence, laws, glares, prayers laced in erasure. They don't ask about my soul—they just write it off.

But I've got something they don't. I've got chosen family, a mirror that doesn't lie, and a voice that knows how to rise.

My queerness is holy.
My truth is my offering.
And I give it back to you,
Love who names me Beloved
even when the world calls me wrong.

I've seen darkness—I've walked through it barefoot. But you, you've been my fire, my protest song, my safe space when nowhere felt safe.

You've lifted me up when shame tried to drown me. You've called me home when home was a dream I hadn't found yet.
I stand today not just surviving—
but sacred,

alive,
and free.

Let them call me wrong.
I know my name.
And Love knows it too.

PSALM 55

Listen, Love—my voice is shaking, like hands holding too much history.
Hear me. Not just my words, but the silence between them. The tired
breath I keep pushing out so I can keep standing.

I'm not okay. Panic wraps around my ribs like vines—tight, unrelenting.
The world feels jagged today. Every headline, every side-eye, every word
spit like acid against bodies like mine—soft, different, real.

I want to run. Disappear into the trees, the ocean, the stars that don't
ask who I love or why I wear my truth so loud.

But it's not strangers that hurt the most. It's the ones who said "I love
you" before their silence became a blade.

You—my friend, my sibling, my kin—
I let you see me, unguarded. And you turned away, not with fists, but
with the kind of absence that breaks bone.

We walked together, dreamed together, sang hymns in pews where I
believed I was safe.
And now, my name tastes like ash in your mouth.

Let me fly.
Let me float above this heartbreak city. Let my soul find sky again.

But no—I'm here. Feet on ground. Heart still beating despite it all.

So I give you this, Love:
my ache,
my rage,
my unraveling.
You, who never turned away
when I said
"I'm queer, I'm trans, I'm me."

You catch what the world drops. You hold what's shattered and call it
sacred.

I cast it all—
this hurt, this hope,
this mess of a life—
into your hands.

Psalm 56

They want me quiet. Want me neat. Want me tucked inside the lines they drew before I was born. Want me afraid of the sound of my own name.

And, Love, sometimes I am.

I hear them—their words heavy like fists, or silence sharp like frost. Their stares feel like fingerprints I never asked for. They twist my joy into something dangerous, my body into a battleground, my love into something I'm supposed to apologize for.

But I will not flinch.

Even though—yeah, I'm scared. Scared of walking home alone. Scared of being too much or not enough. Scared of being remembered only as a headline.

Still, every step I take is a hymn of defiance.

Because you, Love, you keep count of my steps, even the ones that tremble. You've saved every tear like they're prayers, and they are. Every drop is a sacred scream—
I was here.
I mattered.

I believe that. Even when my voice shakes. Even when my heart wants to hide.

I trust you, Love. Not some far-off judge, but the breath inside my breath, the pulse that whispers:
You are holy as you are.

I am not afraid of their shadows. I am light, even when I forget.

This life?
It's mine.
This body?

Mine.
This love?
Divine.

So here's my vow:
I will walk in the fierce light of truth.
I will dance even if they try to chain my feet.
I will love as if it's the last revolution.

Psalm 57

Have mercy, Love—not the kind that pities, but the kind that wraps me
up in denim jackets and calloused hands and says, *you've got this, kid*
when I feel like breaking.

I'm hiding out tonight, but not from who I am. Not from the mirror or
the song in my chest. I'm hiding from the sharp-tongued world that
doesn't know how to hold something so undefinable, so nonbinary, so
alive.

I take cover under your wings—and yeah, I know that sounds religious,
but what I mean is I take shelter in truth, in love that's not ashamed
of me.

I wait for the world to soften, for the sky to remember that it belongs to
all of us, even the ones they call "too much" or "not enough."

They've got arrows for eyes, daggers for words, and their silence?
Louder than bombs.

But I am not afraid. I was born from thunder. I was born to outshine
shame.

Love, you send angels in leather boots and sequined pride, in whispered
you're safe here
and full-volume *come as you are*.

You are my anthem when the world plays fear.

Be exalted, Love—not above the heavens, but in every queer heart that
dares to beat in public. In every trans kid writing poems in the margins
of a world that still doesn't get them.

My heart is steady. My feet, ready. I will rise before the morning, sing
before the light.

Let every song be a protest.
Let every breath be a prayer.

Let every life lived loud be a psalm.

Love, be known in the streets, in the clubs, in the sanctuaries they said weren't for us.

I will praise you with glitter in my veins, with truth in my spine.

I will shout it from rooftops—
Love is love
is love
is survival.

Psalm 58

You, who sit in high places, who write rules in stone and carve names
into gravestones with the ink of your injustice—
do you call this justice?
Do you call this holy?

You sit in your thrones of comfort, pass laws like daggers, and call it
peace.
But we see your hands—stained with the ache of the outcast, the bruises
of the misgendered, the blood of the forgotten.

From the jump, you've been feeding lies like communion bread—bitterness disguised as righteousness, fear dressed up in God-talk.

You hiss at difference like it's poison, but we know it's the antidote to
your flatline faith.

Your words—venom.
Your silence—a song that kills slowly.
You tie stones to our joy and wonder why we drown.

But hear this: We are not afraid of your crooked smiles or the teeth
behind them.

We are the storm you prayed would pass, the thunder you tried to
silence with stained-glass walls.

Break your fangs on our truth.

Let every drag queen, every Black trans woman, every two-spirit elder,
every asexual teen be the roar that undoes your empire.

Let the earth spit back your poison.

Love—
call the light to bear witness. Let the river rise against them. Let justice
flood every street where our blood once soaked the pavement.

Let us dance in their ruin not for revenge but for liberation. For the taste of a dawn where no child is afraid to say their name out loud.

When we rise, and we will rise—
they will know we were never broken, only bending toward the sun like wildflowers refusing to die.

Let our laughter be the anthem. Let our survival be the psalm. Let the world see we were never born to be silent.

PSALM 59

Deliver me, O Love, from those who sharpen their words like switch-blades on sidewalks, from those who eye my joy like it's a threat they can erase.

They gather at dusk, their mouths dripping with fear dressed up as theology, their fists full of stones they swear are commandments.

But I—I wear my truth like armor. My pronouns are prayers. My love is revolution. And I do not run.

See them, God, how they circle, how they plot, how they chant slurs like it's holy liturgy, as if violence ever made them saints.

They don't see me, only the silhouette of who they fear. But I am more than shadow—I am flame. I am the altar and the offering.

Do not let me fall. Rise for me, O Fierce Protector. Be the riot in my lungs when they try to steal my breath. Be the calm in my pulse when they circle, when they shout.

Do not erase them, no—let them see us rise. Let them witness the power of chosen family, the gospel of drag brunches and pride parades that turn mourning into dancing.

Let their laws crumble on the tongues that spoke them.
Let every gate they close be splintered by the laughter of the liberated.

But I—I will sing of your steadfast love. I will belt it on stages, in pews, at protests.
My anthem of survival will echo long after their hate goes quiet.

You, O God of Queer Joy, are my refuge, my safe space, my sanctuary in this skin.

At sunrise, you are the beat in my chest.
At midnight, you are the hands that hold me when the world will not.

You are the harmony when I have no words left.
You are the Love
that will never
never
never
let me go.

PSALM 60

God, it feels like You ghosted us.

Like we showed up to the altar in our finest glitter and You never texted back.

You've seen us—marching with wounds still fresh, loving like rebels who've got nothing to lose, and everything.

But still, we are out here—tired and beautiful, displaced in a land that should have been home.

You've cracked us open, spilled our hope on the pavement, and we're still here—patching up belief with safety pins and pronoun badges and hands held tight in alleyways
where the light still dares to shine.

You gave us a banner to wave high—so why does the wind blow so hard against it?

Why do we feel exiled in pews we helped build?
Invisible in prayers we helped write?

Hear us, Love.
Do not let our hearts become tombstones for dreams that still breathe.

Give us back our joy.
Our chosen names.
Our chosen families.
Our place in the promise we were told was for everyone.

Stretch out your hand—let it be the one that braided our hair before the first day of being seen. Let it be the voice that said,
"You are my beloved. And I meant it."

From every drag ball, from every small-town kitchen table, from every glitter-streaked protest, raise us up.

Let your love be the anthem that drowns out every law that tried to unwrite us.

Let your truth be louder than fear.

Let your justice bequeath the earth to the brave ones who dared to exist outside the lines they told us were holy.

With You, we are not lost. With You, we are the map. And we're not just returning—
we are arriving.

Psalm 61

Hear me, when I'm at the edge of me, when my voice is a flicker, barely breathing through cracked lips and the world is a thunder I cannot quiet.

I am calling from the farthest place I've ever been from love, from safety, from being understood.

Lead me to a rock that doesn't move when I come out, doesn't shake when I speak truth, doesn't flinch when I say I am queer and holy in the same breath.

Let me find a refuge, not just a place to hide but a place to grow.

I want to build a home in Your shadow,
where I can be loud,
where I can be soft,
where I can lay down
every mask they told me I had to wear to be loved.

You've heard me, even when others wouldn't. You've seen me without turning away.
You, who has always held my tears like sacred rain.

You've been my safe space when pews turned cold, when laws turned cruel, when hands meant to bless only bruised.

I am still here.

Let me live in that truth. Let me sing with the lungs You gave me—
the voice they tried to silence, still rising like sunrise through stained glass.

Let me make a vow to joy that no one can break, a promise to love that holds even when
the world doesn't.

I will carry Your light like a banner across every room that ever made me feel too much or not enough.

And I will praise with glitter in my hair, hope in my fists,
and love—
always love—
on my lips.

Forever.

PSALM 62

I have learned to be still—
not because the world is quiet but because I've found a peace they can't
take from me.

My soul waits, not in silence, but in defiance—a hush that says:
I belong. I am love. I am enough.

My safety doesn't come from their approval.
My salvation doesn't wear their name.

I have a God who doesn't misgender me, who doesn't flinch when I kiss
who I love, who doesn't require my apology to offer me grace.

They try to tear me down—words like wrecking balls, laws like cages—
but I am built from holy resilience.

They see me as fragile glass. I am a stained glass window holding
sunlight and shadow,
telling a story that can't be shattered.

Power?
It isn't theirs.
Love?
It was never conditional.

I am not waiting for permission to be whole.

I rest, like a mountain that knows it doesn't need to move to be
magnificent.

Trust—
not in systems,
not in status,
not in the promises of those who forget us.

Trust
in the heartbeat that stayed steady when mine trembled,
in the hands that held me when the church did not.

Love belongs to all.
Love is all.
And I—
I am unshaken.

Psalm 63

God, I'm parched.

Not for water but for belonging that doesn't ask me to shrink.

I wander this wilderness of disapproval, mouth dry from biting back the truth of me.

I've searched for the Divine in all the places they told me not to go— between pride flags and protest chants, in the glint of eyeliner on a boy who won't apologize for beauty.

I've seen You. Not in cathedrals that locked their doors, but in bodies dancing like survival,
in hands that held me when I couldn't hold myself.

And I want more.

More of the kind of love that doesn't flinch when I speak my pronouns aloud, the kind of holiness that calls my queerness sacred, not mistake. My soul thirsts for that.

For you, Love, the one who never leaves when I take off the mask, the one who shows up
to the drag show with glitter in their beard and joy in their eyes.

Your love is better than life—not the life they want for me, the sanitized, straightened, silenced one—but real life, the kind where I can breathe without apology.

So I will praise you with lips that once trembled and now shout with unashamed fire. When I lie awake in the dark, you are the stars that won't burn out.

You are the echo in my chest when I chant, "We're here, we're queer, we won't disappear." You've held me up when I could barely stand. I sing in the shadow of your wings, not hiding, but soaring.

I cling to you, not because I'm weak, but because love was always meant to be mutual.

You hold me fast—not to bind me, but to remind me

I am holy,
whole,
and home.

Psalm 64

Listen, Love—
they're plotting again.

Not with fists, but with whispers, sharp as knives they keep tucked
behind smiles.

They gather in pews, wrap harm in hymns, pray my queerness away like
it's a stain
on the fabric of creation.

They say, "We'll catch them slipping—
trap them with their own joy, twist their laughter into evidence, their
love into sin."

They aim with words, weaponized scriptures, aim for the heart and call
it righteous.

But I'm still standing. Still glowing. Still here.

And you, Divine Resistance, you are the echo in my bones that says:
You are worthy.
You are not a mistake
but a miracle with legs and a pulse and glitter in your soul.

They shoot arrows; you send truth.

Their lies unravel like cheap thread, and what's left?
Their own shame, mirrored back in the faces they tried to erase.

We rise.

We dance louder than their doctrine, love bolder than their fear.

Queer hearts are not your battlefield—
we are your sanctuary,
your revolution,
your witness.

Let every outcast rejoice,
every trans kid find safety,
every ace heart be seen.

We wear our pride like armor,
and Love—
your love—
is the fire
that never burns out.

Psalm 65

Praise rises in our throats, like the first morning breath after a night we thought we wouldn't survive.

You, Holy One, hear us—even the prayers we can't speak aloud, even the ones
wrapped in shame,
wrapped in longing,
wrapped in rainbow flags we're too scared to wave.

You answer not with judgment, but with *welcome*.
You don't ask for credentials, don't gatekeep grace.

You open the door like we've always belonged.

Queer hearts, we gather from every margin, every borderland—exiles turned dancers, misfits turned beloved.

You are the artist of second chances, brushing away guilt like dust from shoulders, offering forgiveness not as a rulebook but as a river, wide enough for all of us.

You, Divine Enby, ground and sky, speak in thunder, but your voice softens to a lullaby for the weary.

Mountains stand like drag queens in stilettos, firm and unmovable, draped in glory.

Seas swirl with the rhythm of pride parades, chaos turned celebration, waves clapping in sync with our joy.

You calm storms—inner ones too, those queer-crushing doubts we carry from pulpits and playgrounds.

You water the earth with the same tenderness you water our souls—and everything blooms.

You crown the year with abundance:
love that doesn't expire,
hope that outlives every attempt to erase us.

Fields shout with wildflowers, meadows dance like we do, unapologetically alive, clothed in truth and glitter. And joy—joy runs like wine, like ink, like a testimony that refuses to be silenced.

Psalm 66

Shout it out, queer fam—
not just a whisper or a polite nod—but a roar, a glitter-bomb hallelujah
from the bones.

All the earth,
all the people,
all the colors,
all the genders
sing along.

Say to the Divine: Your love is fierce, your justice shakes mountains,
your grace undoes chains and heals the bruises we carry from churches
that called us broken.

Everywhere we turn, we see you—in the laughter of drag queens, in the
stories told on front porches by elders who paved the way.

You turned seas into dry land, led our ancestors through impossible
waters
—same way you lead us through bathroom bills and broken systems,
through closets and conversions and into wide open spaces.

We made it. Not untouched, but unbroken.

You let us walk through fire, through silence, through exile. You let the
weight of the world
ride on our backs, but you didn't leave us there. You brought us into
abundance—
chosen family,
safe spaces,
hearts that know we are holy.

We offer you the songs of our survival, the praise of lives uncloseted,
loved, and lit up from within.

Come and hear, you who are still wondering, still hiding, still hurting—
I'll tell you what Love has done for me.

I cried out not in shame, but in hope, and the Holy One leaned in, kissed my fear, and stayed.

Blessed be the One who hears our prayers, who never shuts the door on queer voices, who never stops loving us exactly as we are.

PSALM 67

May the Divine, who made rainbows as promises and protests,
bless us—
bless the broken and brave,
the soft and sharp-edged,
the they/thems and she/hers and he/hims
and all the holy in-betweens.

Shine on us, like glitter in the sun, like a Pride flag in the wind, like
candles flickering for those we've lost and those still finding their way
home.

So that the world might see—
not just tolerance, but love that doesn't flinch,
not just inclusion, but belonging that wraps around like arms after a
long, hard fight.

Let every nation, every people, every kitchen table and street corner sing
of Love's justice—
not just for the loud, but for the silenced,
not just for the famous, but for the forgotten.

Let the earth rejoice—let the land breathe, let the oceans hum, let our
queerness be a hymn the world can't stop singing.

You guide us, not with rules to cage us, but with stories to free us.

Let the people praise you, every language, every dialect, every song in
every key—
praise from the depths of our complex, chaotic, queer hearts.

Abundance spills from your hands—
not just food, but hope,
not just breath, but purpose.

May every generation know they are sacred. May every child grow up
unafraid to be exactly who they are.

And may we all—
blessed and blessing—
keep this love
flowing

Psalm 68

Let the Divine rise up—and let every chain be broken.
Let shame flee like fog burned off by morning sun.
Let fear melt like ice under dancing feet.

Love rides in, not on war horses, but on glitter floats, drums beating
liberation, rainbow flags catching the wind like prayers we forgot we
could say out loud.

Sing, O Queer Ones—make the streets your sanctuary. Make your body
a temple no one can defile. Let every step you take be a psalm of survival.

The Holy One—
protector of trans kids,
mother of drag queens,
father of the femme boys they tried to erase—
sets the lonely in homes of chosen kin, sets the silenced at tables with
microphones and megaphones.

God broke us out of closets like tombs.
God took our hands in the march, held us through the protest, never
left us alone in the alleyways or ER rooms, in church pews or jail cells.

The earth shakes with the pulse of our names finally spoken in love.
The sky pours out like a baptism for those of us who never felt clean.

Blessed be the One who carries our pronouns like poetry, who loves the
loud, the strange, the too-much, the ones who didn't think they'd make
it to morning.

You're the God of the dance floor,
the God of the back row,
the God of the aching and the healing,
and we lift up your name like a battle cry for every soul still fighting to
be seen.

Love is calling.

Queerness is holy.
And we—
we are the parade
of the risen.

Psalm 69

Save me, Love—I'm drowning in the aftermath of being too queer for
their comfort, too real for their systems.
The hate's up to my neck, and I can't breathe in this flood of erasure.

I tried to stand tall, but the ground keeps shifting with every slur, every
law that says I'm less than. My identity's not a debate, but they drag it
through the mud like I'm a storm they can survive by pretending I don't
exist.

I'm weary from screaming, hoarse from praying, eyes swollen from
watching another sibling fall to a world that treats our love like a crime
and our bodies like battlegrounds.

You know the ache, the names they throw, the family that left, the jobs
lost, the nights without a place to feel safe.

Don't let me drown in this.
You're the God of the outcast, the misgendered, the misnamed.
You know my pronouns—say them holy.
You know my heart—call it whole.

I am poured out like protest, like glitter bombs on city halls, like tears
on pillowcases no one else sees.

Let your love rise like a lifeboat, let justice flood this place and wash
away the hate tattoos carved into laws and pulpits.

They mock us—say we're broken, say we chose this pain.
But you, Love, you made us sacred in every shade, every curve, every
defiant breath.

Let them see you in us. Let our survival be the miracle they can't deny.

I will praise you
with my queerness,
with my scars,
with my dance,
with my truth.

For Love listens to the silenced, resides with the rejected, raises the ones
they tried to bury.

And I—I am still here.
Still loving.
Still rising.
Still singing.

Psalm 70

Help me, Love.
Not next week.
Not in time.
Now.
Because the hate's at my door, wearing badges, holding Bibles, passing
laws in the name of God who I know doesn't look like them.

Let those who hunt my joy trip on their own bitterness. Let their
tongues tie when they call me wrong. Let them taste the truth:
I'm divine by design.
Their cruelty?
Unoriginal.

But you—you see me. You made this body nonconforming,
this heart wide open,
this love unapologetic.

To those who celebrate me—who chant in the streets, who write "Love
is Love" in sharpie on bathroom stalls, who call me *they* like it's the
name of an angel—let them shout it loud:
Love wins.
Queer joy is sacred.

I am poor in spirit today, threadbare from trying.
I'm tired, but I'm still here.

Help me, I'm holy.
Hurry.
Let me remember—even now,
especially now—you are the God
who sees me, names me, saves me.

PSALM 71

I run to you, not because I'm weak but because I know power when I
see it—
and it doesn't look like cops or clergy telling me to hush. It looks
like you—
uncontainable,
nonbinary in essence,
refuge and riot both.

Don't let me be erased. Don't let them cancel me with their doctrine
and disgust.

Be my safe house, my chosen family, my hideaway when the world
throws slurs
like stones.

I've been held hostage by shame, but you were the key in my chest,
singing freedom like a song that never forgets its notes.

You've been here since my first breath tasted like survival. You stitched
my name into the cosmos before they tried to assign me a wrong one.

And I've been singing you since playground taunts and bathroom fears,
since lovers left, and churches shut their doors. I've been praising you in
drag and denim, in whispered prayers and shouted protests.

Don't leave me now—I'm seasoned, I'm scarred holy, I've got stories
etched in my bones like psalms tattooed in ink.

Let me speak to the babies—the ones discovering who they are with
trembling hands and bold hearts.
Let me tell them:
You are sacred.
You are loved.
You are not alone.

You've walked with me through closeted nights,
through breakups that cracked my ribs,
through joy that bloomed like glitter after rain.

You?
You are still here.
Still fierce.
Still with me.
Still queer love embodied.

Psalm 72

Give the leaders your justice, not the kind written in stone but the kind tattooed on knuckles, etched in protest signs, the kind that feeds mouths, heals hearts, lets trans kids live.

May they rule with the wisdom of drag mothers and the tenderness of chosen family. Let their laws be lullabies that sing the unhoused to shelter, that wrap hormone therapy in love, that call Black queer joy holy.

Let the people thrive like wildflowers growing through sidewalk cracks, like joy that refuses to be closeted, like the hands of lovers intertwined under judgmental eyes, unashamed.

May every mountain bend to kiss the valleys, and every valley rise with queer dignity and nonbinary fire.

Let the oppressed
be seen,
heard,
named,
celebrated.

Let their blood not cry out from the ground without an answer. Let the systems that fed on them choke on their own cruelty.

Let there be peace that's more than silence. Let it be riot turned refuge, rainbow flags waving over battle-scarred cities, where no child fears to walk home in the skin they love.

May leaders serve, not rule. May they bow low to the goddess of resistance, to the God of the outcast, to the Spirit who queers all power.

Let them protect the lives of sex workers and asylum seekers, the fat, the femme, the disabled, the trans—let every life be sacred.

Let the earth be abundant—not for greed, but for the hungry. Let the rain fall like justice,
not just on the lawns of the wealthy but on the rooftops of public hous-

ing, on the camps of the unsheltered, on stone steps where lovers kiss without fear.

Blessed be the name beyond names, the pronoun beyond binaries, the Love that doesn't fit in stained glass, but lives in our ribcages.

Let every nation not kneel to kings, but to compassion, to truth, to queer liberation. And let the people say: Amen and Hell yes and Love is love is love is love.

BOOK III

PSALMS 73-89

Psalm 73

I've seen them—the ones in suits too tight to breathe, preaching love
with a fist, counting coins instead of hearts, rolling in privilege while we
sleep with one eye open.

And yeah, I almost envied their comfort—the way they wear certainty
like a crown, never doubting their reflection in the mirror, never fearing
for their life just for being alive.

They strut through the world untouched by slurs, untouched by policies that erase my pronouns, untouched by bathrooms where I hold my
breath, wondering if this will be the time someone calls me "abomination."

Their mouths drip power like honey turned poison, their words sharp
like legislation passed at midnight to tell us our love, our bodies, our
breath—don't count.

But then—I step into sacred silence, not the stained-glass kind, but the
kind you find between the beats of a protest chant, between the lips of a
first kiss, between "I'm here" and "I see you."

And I remember: truth doesn't need a throne.

They stand tall, but love is taller. They hoard, but joy is a flood and
we've built arks out of survival.

Their kingdoms crumble in the face of chosen family and dancing in
streets that never welcomed us.

I don't envy anymore. I see clearly now—my queerness is a holy rebellion, my existence a prayer with no end, my body a sanctuary they can't
tear down.

When my heart cracks under the weight of it all, I find You—not in the
rules, but in the rupture, the reclaiming, the rise.

You are not far. You're in every whispered "I love you" said without shame, in every march, every glitter-streaked tear, every safe space carved out of concrete.

You hold me when the world doesn't.
You call me beloved in a voice that has never misgendered me.

I don't want what they have. I've got You. And You are freedom's flame.
You are chosen. You are mine.

Let the world know: Love wins. Always.
And I? I am still here. Still queer. Still holy.

Psalm 74

O Love, how long will they desecrate what we built with our own bodies? How long will they paint bullseyes on our backs and call it holiness?

They storm our spaces—not with swords, but with slurs, laws, and silence—breaking open the doors of safety we dared to call our own.

They raze our sanctuaries brick by brick, say we don't belong
in pews,
in pulpits,
in the pages of Your name.

But we know this: You don't live in stained glass. You are in the shattered mirror, the bathroom stall prayer, the scream swallowed down in Sunday school silence.

They set fire to our histories, erase our names from the lineage of the beloved, but we remember. We remember every hand held in secret, every pride flag carried like a torch through the night.

Our temples stand in the middle of street corners, drag shows, clinic waiting rooms, tiny apartments with mismatched mugs, where chosen family gathers like communion.

You see the wreckage. You walk through it with us—barefoot, bleeding, unafraid.

They say You've forgotten us, but we know You're right here in the chant, in the march, in the kiss that tastes like freedom after a lifetime of hiding.

You made the queer heart strong enough to carry grief and joy in the same breath, to rise when they said we were finished.

You broke the sea in two for the outcast to walk through, and we are still walking.

Smash the chains they tie in Your name. Flip the pulpits. Drown the hate in the flood of our laughter.

You have not abandoned us. We are the revolution's hymn, singing from the rubble, louder than their fear.

Let them tremble. Let them see we are the temple now,
queer and alive,
unburned,
unbreakable,
holy.

Psalm 75

We give thanks not in whispers, but in shouts that echo down back
alleys and protest lines,
in love letters passed beneath bathroom stalls, in every "they" and
"them" spoken like sacred incantation.

Your name, O Justice, is not whispered from high towers, but sung from
lips painted in defiance, sung by those told their voices don't matter.

You say, "In the chaos, I hold steady—the ground, the sky, every trembling heartbeat
you've been told is wrong."

You hold our world when it feels like it's unraveling—when our rights
are on the auction block and we're told to wait, to quiet down, to be
patient while they debate if our love is real.

But you are not patient with oppression. You do not sit silent at their
tables of power. You turn the tables over.

You lift the humble—
the sex workers, the disabled queers,
the trans kids in red states,
the brown and Black femmes
who carry resurrection in their bones.

And you say, "Here is the cup, not of wrath, but of truth." Bitter for
those who've hoarded power, sweet for those who've only ever been told
to drink their shame.

We pour it, too.
This cup of justice.
This cup of love is love is love.
This cup that overflows
with glitter, with grace, with grit.

We lift it high. We raise it in dance halls, in courtrooms, in backyards
where chosen family gathers and God shows up in every laugh.

We will not bow to thrones built on fear. We rise on the strength of every queer elder, every sacred story that dared to survive when survival was the holiest act of all.

We pour the cup, again and again. We are the keepers of this flame, and we will not let it go out.

Psalm 76

In the heart of every dance floor, Your name is holy—not in cathedrals built by kings, but in safe spaces, in pride marches, in whispered I-love-yous that defy the laws of fear.

You are famous in the lands of the overlooked, known in every queer heart that has survived. Your light breaks through hate like glitter through darkness, blinding those who try to keep us invisible.

You silenced the mouths that spat slurs like poison, broke the weapons of systems stacked against us—court rulings, bathroom bans, family rejection—and said, "No more. These are My people, and I will not let them fall."

Your rage is holy, not wrathful but fierce—like a drag queen in six-inch heels refusing to step aside, like a trans elder holding a protest sign that says, "I'm still here. Try me."

When You rise, every power that called us less trembles, because love is loud, and You are the amplifier.

You don't ask for burnt offerings. You ask us to show up—authentic, broken, whole, loud, unapologetically queer. To bring our vows not to temples, but to each other. To love with a love that refuses to die.

You are with the outcasts, the unhoused youth, the asylum seekers fleeing hate, the bodies politicized, the lives debated—and You are done with debate.

You say: "Their lives are not negotiable. Their joy is their weapon. Their breath is a revolution."

We win not with armies—
but with chosen family, with healing, with survival.

We win
by living.

Psalm 77

In the quiet of 3 a.m., when the world is asleep and my heart is a riot—I cry out. Not with polished prayers, but with the cracked voice of a body that knows what it means to beg for peace.

You don't answer the way the world does—with silence, or shame, with doors slammed shut. You answer with breath in my lungs, pulse in my wrist, the echo of every "I made it through" ringing louder than fear.

I remember nights when I couldn't remember why I stayed. Nights when I wondered if You saw me, if anyone did. My hands clenched—not in praise, but in survival. Not in worship, but in trying to hold myself together.

I thought: Is love still real? Does it still choose me? I couldn't find the answer in the mouths of preachers or the pages of doctrine, but I found it in the arms of my people,
in the mirror when I finally said, "You are enough. Stay."

And now—I remember You the way trees remember sunlight after winter, the way scars remember healing more than the wound. You carried me through every "I don't know if I can."

You are not in the sky above the noise. You are in the chaos, in the heartbeat of protest, in the wild laughter after surviving, in the quiet moments we let ourselves feel safe.

You are the God who splits seas so we can walk through, who parts shame with tenderness, who fights for us with joy.

I will remember. Not just You—but the me who didn't give up. The us who didn't disappear.

You are the God who remembers me when I forget myself.
And that is enough.

Psalm 78

Listen. Not to the noise of power, but to the heartbeat of our people—
loud, unruly, soft in the right places, louder where it needs to be.

I've got stories to tell—not sanitized for comfort, but raw and rising.
Tales of nights spent
carving hope into our own skin, of lovers who taught us that our bodies
are temples, not battlegrounds.

We've seen miracles. Not the ones on stained glass windows or in
ancient scrolls—but miracles like coming out and not breaking, like
chosen family that loves us exactly as we are.

They say God split the sea. I say God split closets, broke binaries, shook
pulpits until love spilled out unfiltered and untamed.

We were told to forget—our history, our power, our names.
But we remember.
We sing the songs our foremothers taught us
in secret. We wear the colors they told us to hide like flags of survival.

And yes—we've wandered. Gotten lost in the desert of shame, in the
wilderness of rejection. But we are a people of return—to ourselves, to
each other, to the truth that we are holy.

God fed us—not with bread alone, but with every kiss from our lovers,
every hand clasped in protest, every "I see you" that saved a life.

We failed sometimes. We fell. We forgot our worth.
But grace is tattooed on our skin, inked in stretch marks and laughter
lines, in names we chose because they finally felt like home.

We are the story. We are the ones who keep the flame alive—passing it
from queer elder to queer youth like a promise:
you belong,
you are enough,
you are the miracle.

And we will tell it,
again and again,
until the whole world hears.

Psalm 79

God—They tore our names from their books, burned our flags, mocked our love in the streets like it was shame, not sanctuary.

They painted our joy in blood. Laid waste to the safe spaces, turned altars into battlegrounds, turned laws into weapons.

We are your people, and we have been left bleeding in the gutters while they walked by, quoting verses they never understood.

Our hearts are haunted—not by who we are but by what they did when we dared to live loudly.

We cry out—not for revenge—but for remembrance. Let the world know what they did to us. Let them hear the names of our beloved dead like sacred hymns screamed into the void.

How long, God?
How long will they laugh as we bury another with rainbow roses and fists clenched in rage?

We are not begging for mercy—
we are demanding justice.

Don't forget us. Don't let our tears be wasted. Don't let their hate be the last word.

Let your compassion rise like sparkling smoke, let it cover us like a kiss, like armor, like home.

We are tired of being prey, of being warnings. We are your people—the exiled, the extraordinary, the impossible-to-erase.

Hold us up when the world collapses again.

Give us courage to dance in the ruins, to love in the wreckage, to build from the ashes.

They tried to break us. But we are still here.
Still loving.
Still fighting.
Still holy.

And we will shout your name—not in fear, but in fierce queer joy, until every chain rusts, and every wall crumbles, and every heart remembers we were never meant to be caged.

Psalm 80

Listen, Divine Flame—You who cradle the ones no one else holds, You who shepherd the scattered, gather us in—we are tired of wandering like we don't belong anywhere.

You, who lit the stars with the same fire we carry in our chests, shine on us again.

We've been dimmed by shame that isn't ours, by hands that struck us for loving too loudly, for living too real.

Our joy has been **torn out at the root**, our stories **erased from the scrolls**, but You—You never forgot our names.

Restore us, Flame-Bearer. Let your face light up our shadows, let it burn through the silence they've buried us under.

You planted us like a vine, let us stretch—wild and unapologetic—over fences built to contain us.

We grew. Even when they cut us back, we grew. Even when they called us sin, we bore fruit.

But now? Now we are trampled in their sermons, burned in their laws.

How long will you watch us ache? How long will our tears be the only rain we know?

Don't turn away—return to us. Be the protest in our throats, the shelter we keep searching for.

We are your vine. Your drag queens and nonbinary saints, your trans warriors and asexual healers. We are queer, and we are holy.

Make us shine again—not in spite of who we are, but because of it.

Let them see what they tried to destroy is divine.

And we?
We will not just survive.
We will sing.
We will rise.
We will glow with your light
and never apologize for the brilliance.

Psalm 81

Sing, they said—but only if your voice stays inside the lines they drew.
Praise, they said—but only if your body fits their binary boxes.

But we? We break into chorus with pierced tongues and battle scars,
with voices unfiltered, unashamed.

Strike the tambourine, let the bass line throb like a heartbeat that
refused to stop when they told us we were wrong for existing.

We remember—not Egypt, not chains—but the day we cut our own
ropes, walked out of their cages, and into the wild of our truth.

You said, "I took the weight off your shoulders." And we believed you—
even when churches pressed down harder, even when families chose
silence over love.

You said, "Open your mouth wide, and I will fill it." So here we are,
mouths open not for permission—but for protest songs, for kiss-and-
tell truths,
for queer joy sung at full volume.

But they didn't listen.
Not to You.
Not to us.
Not when we spoke of harm,
Not when we begged for safety,
Not when we just wanted to be held without condition.

So you let them have their gods of gold and fear. But we? We're still here.

You long to fill us with the bread of belonging, with honey pulled from
rocks they swore couldn't nourish.

Feed us.
Free us.
Unshackle our voices until the earth shakes with the sound of our
becoming.

PSALM 82

God walks into the courtroom like a mother who's had enough—
staring down the judges in their robes, gavel in one hand, truth in the
other.

"How long," They demand, "will you keep kissing the boots of tyrants,
while the poor starve and the queer kids sleep in shelters or not at all?"

You call yourselves gods, but you let black trans women die without
names, you let refugees drown with prayers still on their lips, you turn
away kids in rainbow flags as if they're lepers not prophets.

Defend the ones they call disposable. Stand up for the kids in gender
euphoria who just want to live to see next week.

Free the trafficked, the abused, the scapegoated.
Free the nonbinary truth-tellers called "too much" by those who've
never known how to hold a soul that refuses to shrink.

You are gods, but you forgot—your divinity is nothing without justice
pulsing in your veins.

So now the earth shakes.
Not from anger—but from the weight of every silenced voice finally
screaming back.

God says, "I claimed all of you as kin, as co-creators—
but you've forgotten your roots, dancing with power instead of resur-
recting the ones it buried."

Rise up, O Love, queer and thunderous, and judge this world not with
vengeance—but with fire that heals, with rage that rights, with glitter
that refuses to fade.

Psalm 83

Don't be quiet now, Love. Not now. Not ever. They plot with Bibles turned into weapons, laws sharpened like knives to carve us out of history, erase our joy from their stained-glass fantasies.

They gather in secret, but we see them—the ones who whisper that we are abominations, who call queer joy rebellion, trans existence a threat, love—a war crime.

They want to make us myths.
Ghosts.
Forgotten.

But we are the fire that won't be put out. We are Stonewall in every heartbeat, ACT UP in every breath, a revolution in every kiss.

God, scatter their hate like ashes. Make their power crumble like ancient altars no longer fed by fear. Let their pride unravel—like flags ripped from stolen poles and returned to the hands of the ones they tried to silence.

They say they fight in Your name, but they do not know You. They've never seen You in the face of a drag queen praying at dawn, never heard You in the voice of a trans teen singing
their name for the first time.

You are the God of the outcast, the protector of the queer, the pulse in the riot, the whisper in the closet, the shout at the march.

Let them know—not in fear,
but in awe—that You are Love,
untamed, unashamed,
unapologetically queer.

Psalm 84

How beautiful—not the house of God—but the house that we are. Not gold-trimmed ceilings or pulpits carved by gatekeepers, but every chosen family dinner, every ballroom runway, every gender euphoria moment that makes us whisper, "Here, here is where I belong."

My soul doesn't long for a church—it longs for a place where I don't have to shrink to fit someone else's prayer. It longs for a space where "they" is holy, where pronouns are liturgy,
where every breath we take is an act of resistance against those who tried to make our lives a sin.

Even the sparrow finds a nest, the swallow a home for her young—so why did they tell us there's no room in the pews for our love, no room at the table for our truth?

Blessed are the wanderers, the ones who kept walking when the church doors slammed shut. Blessed are the ones who turned exile into sanctuary, who carved altars from heartache and sang hallelujah anyway.

We pass through valleys of shame and bloom gardens there. Every insult we've borne becomes compost—new life rising from the wreckage.

Love shields us.
Truth shines on us.
No good thing is withheld from those who show up as their whole, raw, radiant selves.

O God of Queer Beings, blessed are we—
not when we follow their rules,
but when we trust the fire inside us that says:
"You are sacred, exactly as you are."

PSALM 85

Once, You turned toward us—kissed our chains off, said "You are forgiven" before we even knew we needed grace.

You gathered the scattered, made homes for the disowned, and called it beloved community before the world could weaponize the word.

But we are still waiting, still choking on prayers that taste like ash. We've marched too long to be told to wait for heaven when hell's already at our feet.

Revive us now—not in whispers, but in the roar of protest, in the cry of the youth who come out and come alive.

Let your rage be holy, your justice relentless.
Let truth come, not as a doctrine but as a lover, full of lipstick and scars and non-binary light.

Let mercy and truth make out on the front steps of churches that once exiled them. Let justice and peace hold hands in streets paved with resistance.

We are not asking for crumbs. We are demanding the feast we were always meant for.
And we will not leave until every lost queer soul knows they are divine.

You will plant love in the ground and we will grow it loud—riot gardens blooming in every place they tried to bury us.

Your path, God, is not straight.
It curves like our stories,
it twists like our dance,
it pulses with the heartbeat of those who refused to be erased.

PSALM 86

Hear me, not in the way of polite prayers and folded hands, but in the gut-wrench of a queer kid yelling into a pillow, begging not to be erased.

I am poor in spirit, rich in scars, tired in bones, fierce in love. I carry my worth in the way I keep standing—even after everything tried to knock me down.

Be near. Be real. Be now. Because I'm not sure how many more days I can keep pretending I don't need to be held by something that won't leave when I show my whole self.

You are the safe place when the world tries to legislate my existence out of breath. You are the pulse in my palms when I'm shaking in front of bathroom doors, afraid someone will question my right to be there.

I've cried your name in a thousand ways:
as queer joy erupting,
as trans grief howling,
as nonbinary silence
that still means "I am."

You, Divine One, are no stranger to misfits. You stitched the stars with rebel thread and named the galaxies after those who wouldn't conform.

There is none like You—not in cathedrals, not in courtrooms, not in conversion camps that tried to tell us love is sin.

Your love is riot and refuge. Your love is banner and battle cry. You made us loud, and You never asked us to quiet down.

Teach me Your ways—but don't ask me to be straight in them. Teach me to walk the path in my own damn shoes—heels, boots, barefoot—whatever lets me dance.

I will praise You, not in hymns that erased me, but in the songs we wrote on the back of pain, on the edge of hope, with voices they tried to break.

You, who lifted me from shame's grave—You gave me my name back, called me Beloved and meant it.

The proud still mock, the powerful still crush, but You see me. You know me. You delight in me.

Pour out Your mercy like a flood. Let the world drown in it. Let them see us standing, alive, radiant, queer as thunder, loud as love, unashamed, and holy.

Psalm 87

The Divine laid foundations, not in pews or palaces, but in the breath of outcasts who dared to live, loud and unafraid.

Holy mountain? Try the streets where we march. Try the bedrooms where we love. Try the houses we built from scratch after they burned down our homes.

God loves this city—not because it's perfect, but because we never stopped dancing on its broken stones.

They said: "This one was born there." And they meant it with awe. As if to be born queer, born trans, born wild and radiant was the truest kind of citizenship.

Egypt? Babylon? Call them systems—call them chains—we broke
them all
just by breathing,
by being,
by saying:
We belong here.

They count us now. Not as tokens. Not as quotas. But as founders, as architects of a new world where love is law and shame has no throne.

Every singer, every dancer—they know. This city pulses with us. Her heartbeat is queer. Her streets echo our laughter, our grief, our becoming.

In Her, we were born.
In Her, we rise.
In Her, we write the anthem
of a people who refused to be forgotten.

Psalm 88

O Holy Mystery, I've called your name like a protest chant, like a sob, like a prayer from the edge where the light never quite makes it.
You hear me, right?
Tell me you hear me.

I am full of hurt—not just bones and skin, but bruises shaped like silence, like closets, like rejection letters from churches that said my love was sin.

I am counted with the dead. The forgotten. The ones whose pronouns were misremembered on tombstones or never spoken at all.
My friends have vanished.
My lovers are memories.
Hope is a flickering bulb in a basement where the door's been locked.

You let this happen. You, who knit me in my mother's womb—why does it feel like you unraveled me instead? Was I too much? Too bright? Too loud in my truth?

My days are ash. My nights, long and hollow. Grief has become my bedfellow, and loneliness wraps around me like a second skin.

You say love never fails—then why am I still waiting at the altar of belonging, offering my whole self to a silence that echoes back emptiness?

Do the dead praise you? Do those buried by hate crimes sing? What good is your promise if the queer are erased before their voices are heard?

I am alone. I am drowning. My joy is a ghost I can't catch. My name— forgotten in the mouths of those I love. Even you feel far.

But I'm still here. Still breathing. Still calling your name like a heartbeat that refuses to stop.

O Mystery, if you are love—come find me in this darkness.
Be the light that doesn't ask me to change.
Be the sanctuary where even the shattered are sacred.

Psalm 89

I will sing of love—not the watered-down kind that fits inside wedding cards and cis-het fairy tales—but the kind that rips open skies, pours light into closets, and makes the impossible possible.

Your love, O Mystery, is ancient and infinite, like the first time a trans kid said their name out loud and the stars clapped in response.

You built the world on this love—queer and wild, untamed by dogma or doctrine, a covenant inked in the blood of resistance.

You said, "I will not lie to you. My love will not fail."
We remembered.
We held onto that promise through conversion therapy clinics and Sunday sermons that tried to silence our breath.

You crowned your people with glory, with purpose—but they handed us shame instead,
told us love is conditional, told us we were storms to be calmed.

And yet, we were always rainbows—not just the kind in the sky, but the kind in riots, in chosen families, in bodies that broke binaries and built bridges.

But Mystery—where are you now?
The hate still marches.
The laws still try to erase us.
And your promise feels like it's been folded and forgotten in the back pocket of someone too afraid to live it.

We've been mocked. We've been dragged. Our stories erased from pews and pulpits, as if holiness had a gender, a sexuality, a script.

But I haven't stopped believing. Not in them. Not in their god.
But in you—the God of queerness, the God of liberation, the God who whispered, "You are beloved" before the world learned to hate.

Remember your promise.

Remember us.
Not as mistakes—but as the fierce fire you lit to warm a world that's forgotten how to love.

We are still here,
still singing,
still rising.

BOOK IV

PSALMS 90-106

Psalm 90

You've been our home, even before closets existed, before we carved sanctuaries out of alleyways and whispered names into the dark, hoping someone—anyone—would hear us and say, "You are good."

Before the mountains rose like protest signs, before the first sunrise kissed earth's curves, you were there—
nonbinary and eternal, the they/them of infinity, holding all of us in your expansive, limitless love.

Time means nothing to you—a thousand years are just one drag performance in the great ballroom of your forever. We are dust, they say, but we—queer dust—carrying glitter and grief, sacred and messy in every breath.

We live, we fade, we rage, we die—
but still we rise,
like truth that won't be buried,
like joy that refuses to be banned.

You see our secrets—our desires, our wounds, our dreams drenched in neon and night sweats. You see us. Not as shame, not as sin—
but as sacred.

Teach us, Love, to number our days, to count them not in years lost to hiding, but in kisses stolen beneath moonlight, in hands held across protest lines, in lives claimed loudly, without apology, without erasure.

Let your love break like dawn over all who've known the ache of exile.
Let your pride flag fly in heaven's wind.
Let us know your tenderness—
that mercy that wears combat boots and paints nails and cradles the broken.

Give us joy.
Real joy.
Not just survival, but dancing-in-the-streets joy.

Chosen family reunion joy.
We-are-still-here joy.

Let our lives be your beauty,
our love songs your legacy,
our revolution your praise.

Psalm 91

We dwell in the sacred spaces, the places where we can be true, where our gender doesn't need to be explained, where our love is not a question but a blessing. Under your wings,
we find shelter—not in fear, but in fierce belonging, not in rejection, but in unrelenting love.

We'll say it loud: You are our refuge, our fortress, the God who says, "Come as you are, and I'll show you the kingdom."

We don't fear the storms of the world, the ones who would throw us out for simply existing as we are—because you've always been here, rooted in the soil of our queerness, anchored in the song we sing without apology.

The enemy can try to shut us down, but we rise like fire. No weapon formed against us—no "corrective" love, no law to silence us—can ever break us.
Not with your wings around us.

You will keep us safe in the arms of your care, when the world tries to erase us, when they say our love is dangerous. We know better. We are the storm they fear, and we are the calm they'll never understand.

The young and old, the trans and nonbinary, the queer and questioning —we will find our rest in your arms.

Even when our hearts break, you will gather us,
like a mother hen,
like a father who knows no fear,
like the divine who cannot and will not be boxed in.

When we are lonely, we know you are there, your love is the light that shines in the dark, the truth that cannot be hidden.

We will find refuge in you, not because we are weak, but because we are strong enough to know that our queerness, our love, our existence— is a blessing.

We are never alone.
In the shadow of your love,
we will always find our way home.

Psalm 92

It is a good thing—no, a *holy* thing—to sing love songs in the daylight
and rage anthems under moonlight, to thank the Divine
for this body,
this love,
this breath that refuses to be quiet.

We wake up with joy spilling like glitter down our chests, queer joy—
messy, unapologetic,
loud in the face of those who told us to sit down, shut up, blend in.

We won't.
Our love is sunrise. Our presence is protest. Our laughter cracks stained
glass, and we dance on the shards.

You, O Holy One, made us with hands that sculpt galaxies and hearts
that pulse in sync with rebellion. You didn't make a mistake when you
made us. You called us "good" and "very good" and "damn, look at
them shine."

Our enemies—the ones who clutch their pearls and scriptures they've
weaponized—they won't understand how we thrive in the cracks, how
we bloom at midnight, how we love anyway.

They tried to cut us down, but we grew. Oaks of justice, wildflowers of
pride, we root deep,
bend, but do not break.

In the sacred spaces of our queerness, we bear fruit of resistance, leaves
of healing for every kid who thought they were alone. For every soul
who whispered prayers from closets and bathroom stalls, we are the
answer:
you are not alone.
You never were.

We are planted in love, rooted in divine defiance, growing louder,
stronger, freer—

singing songs at dawn to a God who always saw us,
loved us,
named us enough.

Psalm 93

The Divine reigns—not with iron fists but open hands, soft palms
where we trace the map of liberation.

God wears majesty like a hand-stitched cloak of denim and silk,
threaded by drag queens, trans prophets, nonbinary mystics who know
divinity isn't binary, and glory doesn't fit in boxes.

Power wrapped in sequins and scars, righteousness that smells like sweat
and sage, we walk holy runways lit by the fire of being fully seen.

The world? It's been flooded before—
with hatred,
with laws that try to erase us,
with voices that call us "abomination"
and think love can drown under the weight of fear.

But the waters rise—and so do we.
Louder than the tides of bigotry, louder than the waves of shame they
tried to bury us under—
we are thunder, storm-birthed and radiant, our lives the sound of
refusal.

God is mightier. Mightier than the storm in our chest when we first said
"I am" and meant it.
Mightier than every pulpit spitting sermons like knives. Mightier than
closets, than graveyards, than silence.

God is trans joy.
God is nonbinary peace.
God is queer love
on a Sunday morning with glitter on the communion bread and
pronouns on the name tags.

This holiness? It's forever.
Not just for yesterday's saints, but today's warriors, today's lovers and
creators who know that sacred doesn't mean straight, and eternal
doesn't mean exclusion.

Holiness is now.
Holiness is us.
Forever.
Forever.
Forever.

Psalm 94

O Justice, O Love, show up.
Show out.
Make yourself known like a protest in the heart of oppression, like truth
on a mic turned up to 11.

The power-hungry keep their boots on the necks of the beloved.
They legislate hate, write grief into law, and call it "order."
But we've seen this before—
this endless cycle of erasure.

They gaslight the grieving, murder the innocent with systems, then ask
why we are angry.
They think our tears are weakness, our joy is a phase, our love—an
affront.

But Love is louder than law.
Love is louder than lies.

God, do You not see? Do You not hear when they chant Your name
while striking us down? Do You not rise when we fall, when we scream,
when we refuse to bow to anything but truth?

You taught our hands to rise, our voices to resist, our bodies to march,
to dance, to break and rebuild a better world.

You are not neutral. You are not silent. You do not sit on the sidelines
while the sacred are slaughtered by indifference.

You are the heartbeat of defiance, the architect of uprising, the fire in the
eyes of the drag queen who refuses to hide, the calm in the voice of a
trans child speaking their name for the first time and knowing it is holy.

They think we will disappear.
They think fear is enough.
But they forgot: we are divine thunder, queer resurrection, grace with a
backbone, mercy that bites back.

We are the dream You never stopped dreaming—
not broken, not erased. We are Your justice, in skin and wearing sparkles,
in pronouns and pride, in every act of love that refuses to bow.

Let the wicked tremble.
We are coming.
And You—
You are with us.

Psalm 95

Come on—let's make some holy noise. Let's shout to the God who carved queerness into the cosmos like constellations of defiance.

Let's raise our hands, clap with nails painted in protest, feet stomping in rhythm with every ancestor who dared to love loud.

The Divine is not fragile.
Not offended by our joy.
Not rattled by our gender.
God holds oceans in their palms—do you really think your pronouns threaten Them?

The mountains bow to a Creator who made us fluid,
made us fierce,
made us kin
to the sunrise and the riot.

So we kneel—not in shame, not in silence, but in reverence for a God who knows the curve of our spine, the tremble of our grief, the courage in our kiss.

O People, don't harden your hearts. Don't forget how Love led you out—
out of closets,
out of fear,
out of spaces that told you, you were too much, not enough, unworthy.

You've wandered. You've wept. You've wondered if joy was made for people like us.
It was.

Don't let the bitterness of their rejection rob you of the truth: you are holy. you are held. you are the Beloved's own.

And this God? Not some stone idol wrapped in purity politics, but a living, breathing liberator who sings in our accents, marches in our parades, loves in our bodies.

So come on—shout it. Sing it. Dance it.
We are not forgotten.
We are not forsaken.
We are the wild hymn
they never saw coming.

Psalm 96

Sing a new song—not the hymn they forced down your throat, but the melody you found in the mirror, the harmony of your name whispered like a prayer you finally answered.

Sing it loud. Sing it glittered. Sing it in your chosen pitch, your holy tone, your full-throated yes to being fully, freely unapologetically alive.

Let the earth hear—let the trees sway to the rhythm of nonbinary praise, let the oceans echo with the laughter of drag queens and the tears of lovers who dared to hold hands in public spaces that once hissed like vipers.

Declare it:
we are here.
Queer joy is sacred.
Our stories are scripture.

The Divine doesn't need a stage. Doesn't need permission. Doesn't need the approval of pews lined with judgment. God dances in gay bars, in protest lines, in the quiet embrace
of two souls who never thought they'd be safe.

Let the heavens rejoice—because justice is coming, not in suits and gavels, but in pronouns respected, rights protected, bodies loved as they are.

Let the fields shout. Let the sky wave trans flags like holy banners. Let the church bells ring
in queer keys. Let every closet door burst open with angels singing you are free, you are free.

The God of the cosmos does not come to silence us—
but to amplify our liberation song.

So lift your voice,
your painted face,
your weary feet—
Sing.
We were born
to sing.

Psalm 97

God reigns—not on some golden throne in a palace of patriarchy, but in the marrow of every misfit who refused to bow to the empire of conformity.

Let the earth rejoice—let every drag stage and protest march become cathedrals.
Let the mountains melt like wax under the heat of holy fire called self-love.

Clouds and thick darkness surround Her—
because truth isn't always polite, and justice doesn't arrive in silence. It comes roaring, screaming, demanding a world where we are not just tolerated, but celebrated.

Lightning slices through the sky—a strobe light on the dance floor of creation, where bodies move like prayers, where every spin and dip defies erasure.

The earth sees and trembles—not in fear,
but in awe of the power we wield when we love without shame.

The heavens proclaim Her righteousness, and every heart that ever dared to beat out of rhythm with the rules—
knows it.
Feels it.
Embodies it.

Idols of hatred, of rigid binaries and locked bathroom doors—they crumble.
Queer joy is the wrecking ball, and love is the anthem on the lips of the survivors.

You, beloveds, you who bear the scars of battle, the ones who loved when love was dangerous—you are light.

Light poured out like honey.
Light that dances in every color.
Light that refuses to be dimmed.

Rejoice in that.
Rejoice like a prism in a sunbeam.
Rejoice like chosen family around a table where no one has to hide.

God is with us—
in our rage,
in our tenderness,
in our resistance,
in our radiant Queerness.

Psalm 98

Sing a new song—not the old hymn written by hands that never touched your truth, but a song with hips that sway and fists that rise.

Sing like revolution is your birthright. Because it is.

God has done wonders—like waking up in a body you're finally learning to love, like finding a name that fits like a second skin, like kissing someone and not apologizing after.

Her right hand—calloused from building safe spaces out of broken churches and burn-out hearts—has worked salvation in the form of chosen family, midnight text check-ins, and hands held tight in protest lines.

The Holy One has remembered Her love—
not the love that demands we shrink, but love that expands to hold every gender, every pronoun, every sacred 'they/them' and 'call me by this name.'

Let the whole damn earth shout—
drag queens,
and leather daddies,
and trans kids
writing poems on bathroom stalls—
every voice a battle cry of joy.

Let the sea roar with us. Let rivers clap in time with our heartbeat, mountains singing backup vocals to the melody of our unbreakable selves.

Because God is coming—not to judge with wrath, but with justice that loves us back into being, justice that queers the very word 'righteous,' justice that kisses our scars and says, "You are holy."

So sing.
Loud.
Off-key.

In drag.
In truth.
In rebellion.

Sing the kind of song
that sets the world
on fire
with love.

Psalm 99

The Holy reigns—not in thrones of gold, not in laws that cage love, but in the riotous, radiant heartbeat of every queer soul who refuses to be erased.

Let the people tremble—not in fear, but in awe, because the Divine has never been straight-laced, never been small enough to fit in anyone's closet.

The Holy is enthroned among us—in drag queens draped in glory, in lovers holding hands in defiance, in trans bodies sacred as scripture, in the ones who know that holiness is not about who we are told to be, but about how fiercely we love.

Let them praise your name, not because they were told to, but because they have seen your justice unfold in the hands of those who refused to stay silent.

Mighty One, you have always been on the side of the oppressed, parting seas for the outcast, lifting up those who have been cast down.
You spoke through prophets,
through poets,
through the ones whose voices were never meant to be heard
—and still, you speak.

So we lift our hands, our hearts, our full, untamed selves before the Holy, before the One who is and always has been too vast, too wild, too free to ever be anything but Love.

Psalm 100

Make a joyful noise—not the kind they taught you in pews lined with fear, but the kind that erupts from drag brunches, from Pride parades, from the trembling hands of someone saying, "I'm finally free."

Serve Love with gladness—with glitter smeared across your cheeks and a heartbeat that doesn't apologize for dancing off-beat. Come into Her presence like you belong there— because you do.

Know this truth: God made you in every stretch mark and curve, in every binder and stubble, in every trans body and fluid spirit. You are not a mistake. You are not too much. You are not too loud. You are Theirs.

We are Their people—tattooed and pierced, soft and hard, broken and blooming. Chosen family of the Divine, herded not by force, but by fierce, unconditional love.

So enter Their gates—not with shame, not with silence, but with thanksgiving that screams: "I made it. I'm here. I'm enough."

Bless Their name—the name that lives in every queer kiss, every name reclaimed, every voice rising against erasure.

For They are good—not because They are untouchable, but because They touch us in every act of justice, in every moment of becoming, in every sacred "they/them" that reclaims holiness.

Their love endures—
like our joy,
like our rage,
like the stories we tell
so the next queer kid knows they're not alone.

Psalm 101

I will sing of loyalty and justice—but not the kind written in court-rooms that banned my love, not the kind that silenced pronouns and called it order.

I will sing of a new justice—where drag queens are prophets, trans kids are sacred, and love isn't a crime but a covenant.

I will walk with integrity, even when the road refuses to see me. Even when my body is policed, my voice dismissed, my worth interrogated.

I will not let hatred rent space in me.
Not fear,
not shame,
not the lies I once believed when they said I had to be smaller to be loved.

No.
I keep my eyes on love that liberates.
I swipe left on hate.
I unfollow cruelty.
I choose the ones who build up, who celebrate, who refuse to sell their soul for approval.

I will not tolerate the whisper campaigns, the gossip that kills a thousand small cuts. Keep your drama. Keep your bigotry. I've got joy to tend. I've got kin to protect.

My house, my heart, my chosen family—we are a sanctuary.
No TERFs, no fascists, no haters in my holy space.

I rise every day to love loud. To center the outcasts. To dance with the ones who were told they didn't belong—but knew better.
Who made belonging their birthright.

I will not waver. I will not wait for permission to shine. This is my vow.
My glitter-drenched promise.
To walk proud,
to love big,
to fight soft.

Psalm 102

Hear me, O Queer Love, when I can barely whisper. I am unraveling like seams too worn to hold.

Don't turn away when I am this scorched and hollow. I'm burning, but not the good kind—not protest fire, not pride parade spark—this is grief fire, ash in my lungs, hope flickering like it's out of battery.

Days melt into panic, nights stretch into static.
I forget to eat,
forget to feel,
just scroll through the wreckage of the world and wonder if I'm next.

My bones ache protest songs. My skin is parchment, written in scars no one sees.

But You—Divine Queer Flame—
You are not undone by my brokenness.
You don't flinch at my mess.
You make altars out of my ache, turn tears into holy water.

You are the one who stays when everyone leaves. The one who hears my DMs when I text the void.

The one who says: "I am here, in the ash, in the rage, in the breathless hush before you rise again."

You are not a god of perfection. You are a god of persistence. You sit in the ruins with me and call them sacred ground.

You love me not despite my unraveling, but because of it. Because I dared to live, to resist, to keep breathing when everything said stop.

My story won't end here. My name is written in the stars that refuse to burn out.

You are rebuilding me with gold seams and queer fire, for generations who will rise from this ash and dance.

Psalm 103

Bless the Queer Divine, O my whole being—this body they tried to shame, this heart they tried to silence, this spirit they tried to cage.

Bless every scar, every pronoun declared, every dance floor redemption, every kiss that felt like home.

I will not forget how Love pulled me from the pit, stitched me back with glitter and grace, said, "You are not broken. You are becoming."

You crowned me with chosen family, fed me truth when the world fed me fear. You renewed my youth like a trans phoenix, rising from the ash of erased histories.

You are not the god of shame. You are the God of drag shows, of basement churches where queer kids find sanctuary in song, of hands held under protest banners.

You work justice for every beloved cast out, every heart called an abomination when it was a revolution.

You showed yourself to Moses, but you show yourself to us in transition timelines, in chosen names, in the wild holiness of living true.

You are compassion that marches, mercy that riots for joy, slow to anger but quick to dance.

You don't hold grudges. You don't keep receipts of my failures. You toss them into the skyand say, "Let's try again, beloved."

You know how fragile I can be—you know I am made of stardust and scars. But you don't pity me. You honor me. You see every breath as a psalm.

Your love stretches from eternity to eternity, wrapped around every queer ancestor, every youth figuring it out with shaky hands and a fire in their eyes.

You are sovereign not with fear, but with tenderness. You reign in safe spaces, in truth circles, in every whispered "Me too" that shatters silence into song.

Bless the Divine, all you queer angels, you gender-blessed and love-loud creatures.

Bless the Divine, you drag queens, you ace icons, you butch prophets, you nonbinary mystics.

Bless the Divine, O my soul—for I am alive, I am loved, and that is holy.

Psalm 104

Oh Divine—they/them of the galaxies, how majestic your drag stretched across the universe, draped in nebula silks, crowned with comets, spinning planets like ballroom vogues through infinity.

You wrapped yourself in light, a shimmer-cloak stitched with the aurora's breath, and you *walk* on the wings of wild winds—fierce and free, nonbinary in every step.

You laid the foundation of the earth like a queer architect who *knows* that difference is holy, that color and curve are sacred design.

You dressed the mountains in majesty, let rivers flirt with valleys, made the oceans dance with sky. Even the thunder is a love song—loud, unapologetic, queer as hell.

You send rain to thirsty lands, to parched hearts, to dusty closets. You make the grass grow for the wild deer and the city queer. You give wine to gladden hearts, oil to anoint every gender-blessed brow, bread to sustain the revolution.

Every tree of the field claps their branches, every bird in the sky sings in nonbinary notes. Even lions cry out to you in their own tongue, and you meet them in all their holy hunger.

When you breathe, everything breathes—from whale to worm, from star to stone, from pronoun shift to sacred kiss.

And when you withdraw, we return to dust—glitter dust, rainbow ash, dancing atoms that once knew how to love without fear.

Oh Queer Creator, your works are many, your heart expansive, your love limitless. You play with Leviathan like a drag queen spinning joy on the sea's dancefloor.

We are all fed from your open hands, queer and straight, cis and trans, neurodiverse and divine in our own unique pulse.

May my song be a love letter to you—
a protest chant,
a bedroom whisper,
a full-throated hallelujah in glitter paint.

Let my breath be praise.
Let my queerness be prayer.
Let my life be proof
that the cosmos is queer as hell—and holy too.

Psalm 105

Sing out—not soft, not shy—LOUD,
with voices sharpened by survival, tender from kissing truth in the face
of fear. Call out their name—the Holy One, They/Them/All—whose
heartbeat thunders through marches, vigils, and love songs lit by candle-
light and revolution.

We remember. We carry the stories—stitched into leather jackets,
tattooed in ink and scar, told in basement bars and church pews we
reclaimed with our bodies.

The Holy moved through us, queer and shimmering, called Abraham
from comfort, Sarah from barrenness, and *still* their promise bore fruit
—like us, unexpected and radiant, divine contradictions breathing free.

They wandered, we wander, but not lost—pilgrims of love, nomads of
resistance. And God—they—them—walks with us still, in drag queens
and dyke marches, in chosen family and ballroom nights.

God sent us liberators—the Moses of stonewall, the Miriam of song,
voices rising against every Pharaoh that dared to silence our existence.

Plagues of injustice fell—
closets cracked,
chains broke,
walls shook,
and we
came out—
not just into daylight, but into ourselves.

We remember the manna of kindness, the water of survival gushing
from desert places—from safe spaces to late-night calls, from therapy
couches to back-alley kisses that kept us *alive.*

The Holy One remembers, too—the covenant written not on stone but
on skin, on scars, on every "they" that was misnamed, on every "we"
that refused to bow.

Praise the Queer Creator, whose love does not expire, whose promise queers time, breaks chains, makes home out of wandering.

We are the memory.
We are the song.
We are the story still being sung into fierce, fabulous freedom.

Psalm 106

Praise to the Fierce One, whose love is louder than the shame we've been taught to carry. Whose mercy stretches wider than gender binaries, whose grace refuses to stay silent in the face of oppression.

We remember. We messed up—yes. We doubted our own worth, believed the lies tattooed into our childhoods—"too much, too wrong, too queer."
We tried to blend in, to disappear, to survive.

But survival cost us parts of ourselves—sacrificed on altars of acceptance that never came. We forgot who we were. Tried to worship what could never love us back:
approval, conformity, the hollow safety of silence.

Still, the Holy never left us. They raged with us. Wept beside us. Called us out of closets, out of shame, into light that felt like fire.

Our ancestors danced through deserts, fell, rose again. We, too, have wandered—into the arms of lovers and heartbreak, into movements that saved us, into nights where we thought we'd never see dawn.

But grace chased us down—in protest chants, in chosen family dinners, in the softest "I see you," when we most needed to be seen.

We've been rescued more times than we can count.
By queer elders,
by trans siblings,
by our own strength when no one else showed up.
That's holy, too.

And now we rise—from ashes, from erasure, from systems built to forget us. We are the testimony, the proof that love is mightier than hate, that queer joy is divine rebellion.

Bless the Holy One who holds our scars like sacred scripture.
May we never forget the God who never forgot us.

BOOK V

PSALMS 107-150

Psalm 107

Let the reclaimed say so—those exiled by fear, by family, by faith that shunned instead of sheltered.

Let the rescued shout it—queer voices rising like waves, like protest songs, like gospel that's been waiting centuries to be sung by *us*.

We were lost. In systems that spat us out, in closets that became coffins, in pews where we bowed our heads and prayed to disappear.

But Love heard.
Love *moved*.
Love broke open the sky and sent lifelines in the form of chosen family, in the form of glitter and fire, in the form of truth that refused to die.

We cried out. In hospital beds, on street corners, into pillows soaked with "why me?"
And the Holy replied: "Because you are mine. Because your heartbeat is holy rhythm. Because this world needs
your light,
your fight,
your fierce, fabulous,
unbreakable soul."

Some were chained—to shame, to addiction, to names that didn't fit. But the chains snapped when we spoke our truth aloud. When we danced under moonlight, claimed our pronouns, loved boldly in the face of death.

Some wandered in deserts of doubt, parched by promises that never quenched. But Love built rivers in our wilderness, set tables for us in the presence of every enemy that said we didn't belong.

And we belong. Oh, we belong in cathedrals and kitchens, in board-rooms and back alleys, in every sacred place we set our feet down.

Let the earth hear us—Love is not a closet. Grace is not a straight line. We are salvation's song—imperfect, radiant, unapologetically queer.

So we tell it:
the storms we survived, the hands that held us, the lips that kissed us
whole. We tell it because our lives are psalms now. Because the story isn't
finished. Because the flood of grace is still rising—and we are the tide.

Psalm 108

My heart is a wildfire, steady and ready—strapped in stilettos or boots, glitter-smeared or scar-clad—I rise before the light, singing songs that crack ceilings and melt shame into art.

I will not wait for permission to praise. My body is holy, my pronouns divine, my breath a blessing to every space I enter.

Awake, soul!
Awake, tongue!
Awake, love that won't be tamed!
Let the dawn hear us, let the night echo back—we are *here*, queer and alive, unbroken.

I will shout it across timelines, across borders and binaries, into pews and parliaments—Love wins. Love *already* won when we danced in defiance, when we kissed without fear, when we dared to hold each other and believe we were worthy of *every* drop of grace.

You, Holy One, are the pulse in our revolution. You are the banner we carry when the streets burn with protest, when laws try to silence our joy.

Stretch out your hand over every nation that says we are too much. Let them see that our fire is your fire—justice tattooed on our arms, hope inked in our veins.

We march not just for survival, but for abundance, for the day when every queer kid can breathe easy, when "chosen family" means *family*, period.

Holy One, through you we blaze. Through you we kick down the doors of hate. With you we shine, never dimming, never shrinking, always rising—
bright as the stars we were born from.

Psalm 109

They spit lies with polished tongues, smile daggers behind closed doors,
write laws that tighten nooses—I know this dance.
I've heard their slurs—soft as sermons, sharp as knives—but I won't
bow, not to their God who looks nothing like love.

They call me wrong, a phase, a sin with a face. They pray me silent, pray
me straight, pray me erased—but love don't play that game.

Let them curse. I bless.
Let them bind. I break free.
Let them mock my light—I shine louder.

Holy One, my pulse and protest, my refuge in every storm of slurs—
don't stay silent. You've seen me hunted, haunted, hollowed out by the
weight of their hate.

Lift me up from this ash heap, wrap your arms around my scars, paint
me in dignity, wrap me in glory like a battle flag.

They tried to cancel my worth, but I was written in your own hand—
with a glitter gel pen, with calligraphy carved from survival.

I stand in every street they said I didn't belong. I live in every breath they
tried to choke. I dance on the graves of their shame.

Let them watch me
blessed
beloved
bold—queer to the bone, and still holy.

I'll give thanks, not in whispers—but in thunder.
I'll shout your name in drag halls, in courtrooms, in churches that
tremble at the sound of truth.

You don't just save me.
You see me.
You stand by me in the fire and say, "This one? This one is mine."

Psalm 110

The Holy One whispered like revolution at midnight: "I crown you.
Now rise."

Not in the way kings do—power-hungry, iron-fisted—but in truth's full
glow, fierce and unafraid, draped in every color they tried to bleach from
your soul.

Enemies?
They'll watch. Footstools beneath your march. Not because you
crushed them, but because you lived, louder than their hate, more alive
than their rules.

You wear holiness like sequins and scars—
reflecting light,
defying gravity,
dancing past borders they swore were sacred.

You don't need their permission to be divine.

You've been priest and prophet since your first breath—
and this altar?
It's yours.
Your hands, anointed by fire and survival, bless every rebel who thought
they were alone.

You stand with strength born not from conquest,
but from coming out,
again and again, in a world that calls your love a threat.

Your reign is tenderness in a cold world,
mercy in the face of cruelty.
Your justice isn't punishment—
it's liberation.

You are chosen. Not in spite of your queerness—because of it.
The Divine sees you
as whole,
as radiant,
as crowned.

Let them write laws.
Let them build thrones.
You've already won.

Psalm 111

I will praise—not quietly, not in whispers—but loud, unashamed, in the gathering of my people, my beautifully, boldly queer kin.

Our stories—etched in stretch marks, tattoos, battle scars, and laughter too wild for pews to contain—are sacred text.

The works of the Divine?
They are us—
bodies kissed by grace,
minds fierce with wonder,
souls unbreakable,
even after they tried to rewrite our names out of holy things.

Everything the Holy One touches is laced with justice, rooted in love that doesn't flinch at who we are or who we're becoming.

Our liberation is not a favor—it's a promise carved in the stars, sung in the cries of every soul told they were too much or not enough.

God fed us when the world withheld.
Gave us breath when laws stole safety.
Called us beloved before we called ourselves that.

Queer history is holy history. A record of defiance woven brilliantly,
in pronouns reclaimed,
in families chosen,
in prayers screamed between heartbreak and hope.

God's covenant is not reserved for the palatable. It's inked in the pulse of every outcast who dared to dance anyway.

Truth? It doesn't fade. Neither do we.

Praise isn't just hallelujahs—it's protest signs, marches in rainbows, midnight phone calls saving lives, loving ourselves against every odd.

Holy awe is the first breath after coming out.
It's finding your reflection and not apologizing.
It's calling this body home.

This praise is the beginning of wisdom.
And baby, we are wise beyond measure.

PSALM 112

Blessed are the ones who live loud, love real, and lean into justice with calloused hands and every growing hearts.

They aren't afraid to name the systems,
to disrupt the silence,
to love in ways that heal wounds and shatter chains.

Their descendants—blood or chosen—will carry legacy like fire in their bones. Revolution in their veins. Courage in their breath.

Abundance isn't what they own—it's who they are. Rich in kindness, in fierce love, in sacred defiance.

In the darkest nights, they shine—
stars wrapped in skin,
truth wrapped in tenderness.
Unshaken by storms because they *are* the storm.

Justice is their anthem. Not performance—but pulse. A rhythm of care, compassion, and calling out harm without losing tenderness.

They won't be moved. Not by hatred, not by laws, not by pulpits that call their love sin.

Their hearts? Anchored in freedom. Eyes wide with hope. Feet dancing toward liberation with every step.

They lend without fear. Give love without measuring. Hold space for those still finding their voice.

Their names are echoed in every story of survival. Their faces—mirrors for those who thought they'd never belong.

The wicked—those who cling to power, who hoard love, who build walls—they tremble.

Because light like this—queer light, unapologetic light—can't be snuffed out.
It exposes,
it uplifts,
it liberates.

And this light? It blesses everything it touches.
Including you.
Including now.

Psalm 113

Rise up, queer hearts, trans bodies, nonbinary dreams, dragged through
dust and still shining—you are not forgotten.

Let every mouth chant the names of those cast out—
and lift them higher than shame could ever reach.

From the broken pews to the neon-lit streets,
from protest lines to whispered prayers—
Praise rises from queer lips, from chosen kin.

The Holy? They/She/He/Ze—is not perched in far-off heaven, but
kneeling low, in alleyways and hospital rooms, in hearts wrapped in
pride flags and grief.

The Divine's glory is us—holding each other through the night, raising
joy from the ashes of hate.

Who is like this God?
Who *sees* us—not as sinners, but as miracles still unfolding.

They stoop low, into our mess, our chaos, our survival—and lift us from
the dirt, not to shame us, but to crown us.

They sit the broken,
the unloved,
the misgendered,
the excommunicated—
at the table, head of the feast.

The barren—not only of womb, but of hope—
are given a house, a name, a song to sing.

From sunrise to sunset, this truth stands:
We are not forsaken.
We are lifted,
celebrated,
held.

The world may try to erase us.
But God?
They write us in bold.
In neon.
In fire.

Psalm 114

When our people broke chains—marched out of closets, out of pulpits
that bruised, out of pews that spat silence—the world shuddered.

Love cracked the ground open. Stone churches trembled. Systems shook
under the weight of our truth.

Sea fled—not from fear,
but to make way for our fierce procession.
Mountains skipped—yes, danced—
as we claimed the streets in rainbow riot.

What power made waters peel back? What voice made rocks tremble?
It wasn't wrath—
it was freedom.
It was us.

Earth, do you feel it? Do you quake with holy rage? Do you rise with the
march of every trans kid finding their name and speaking it out loud?

Tremble, o power, before the God who chooses
the forgotten,
the exiled,
the queer and beloved—and births liberation from stone.

This Holy One—they take stone hearts and water them with justice.
They turn erasure into a flood of presence.
We are here.
We are home.

Psalm 115

Not to your gold-plated gods, not to the polished pulpits, not to their
fame, their fake smiles, their sanctimonious silence
—but to Love, unapologetic, goes all the glory.

Why do they ask, "Where is your God?"
We say: right here—in the kiss held in public, in the chosen name
spoken bold, in drag queens blessing bread with grace.

Their idols? Dead things. Silver, gold, power hoarded, doctrines dry as
bones,
eyes that never see us,
mouths that spit hate but call it love,
hands that don't heal,
feet that won't walk with us.
And those who worship them? Hollow.

Their hearts echo with fear, afraid of freedom, afraid of bodies alive in
their truth.

But we? We trust in a God who *breathes* through resistance,
wraps us in riot and rainbows, blesses our becoming.

Queer ones—you are held.
Trans saints—you are shielded.
Aces, enbies, lovers of all genders—They are our refuge.

Let them bless us all:
young and old,
scarred and sacred,
those still healing,
those still fighting,
all held in the wild grace of love.

Our God? Not theirs.
Ours lives in the margins, in alleyway baptisms, in whispered prayers
that sound like protest chants, in love that is love that is love.

We will praise,
we will rise,
we will not be erased.
From every corner, every closet flung open, we dance in divine defiance.

Psalm 116

I love you, Holy One,
because you have heard me—
not just the prayers whispered in safe spaces,
but the silent screams in the night,
the shaking breath before speaking my truth out loud.
You have always bent your ear toward me,
catching every word, every tear, every longing.

So I will keep calling,
even when the world tries to silence me,
even when they tell me I am too much or not enough.
You are not like them.
You have never turned away.

How can I repay a love like this?
A love that held me when my own reflection felt like a stranger,
that stayed when the church doors slammed shut behind me,
that saw me not as a mistake, but as a miracle.

I will live my truth boldly—
this is my offering.
I will claim my joy without apology—
this is my praise.

I will stand with the trans kid rejected by their family,
the queer elder who's outlived too many friends,
the Black and brown voices silenced in the pews,
the disabled and neurodivergent fighting to be seen,
the immigrant searching for home,
the sex worker, the addict, the one who's been told they are unworthy of
grace.

And I will lift my cup to the sky,
knowing you are the One
who has always called us beloved,
who has always filled us to overflowing

Psalm 117

Hey world—listen up!
Every nation, every tongue, every person who's ever felt too much or
not enough—this is for *you.*

Praise the Love that *sees* us, not just tolerates, but *celebrates,*
wraps us in affirmation and fire,
genderfluid grace,
nonbinary brilliance,
lesbian laughter,
trans tenderness,
asexual autonomy,
all of it holy.

God's love? It's *louder* than hate, *wider* than binaries, *deeper* than
dogma. It doesn't flinch at pronouns, or fumble over names. It is solid,
fierce, forever.

Queer joy is worship.
Queer love is sacred.
We live. We love. We praise

Psalm 118

Let me tell you—I almost didn't make it.
The nights got long. The world sharpened its teeth.
And still—Love held me.

I was surrounded, boxed in by bigotry, gasping under doctrines that
called my body a mistake.
But queerness?
Queerness *is deliverance.* Love cracked the sky open and I walked free.

God is not some distant tyrant—God is the breath in our protest songs,
the sweat of drag queens dancing for their lives,
the ink in our love letters, the fierce pulse of chosen family.

I cried out—not just once—and they tried to erase me.
But the stone the builders rejected—the trans kid kicked out,
the ace teen silenced, the nonbinary soul erased—
WE. ARE. THE. CORNERSTONE.
And we are building a world that holds us all.

This is the day
we survive,
we rise,
we resurrect.
We love in defiance.
We live in color.
We are the kin-dom come.

So dance, my loves. Shout your names. Lift your scars. Sing like salvation is a kiss from your truest self.

Love wins.
We're proof.
We're the resurrection and we're not going back.

Psalm 119

I breathe in your words, not the ones weaponized by pulpits
but the ones etched in stars, in back-alley handholds, in the whisper of
"you are worthy" at 3am when the mirror lies.

Blessed are we—not in perfection but in survival.
In binding wounds with glitter,
in crafting love out of exile,
in saying: *this body is mine* and *this life is holy.*

Cut through the noise, the hate in hymns that never saw my face.
Your truth is not a prison—
it's the key, the cracked door, the open sky.

Dykes, drag queens, demi-loves and dreamers—
we are your psalm,
we are the ink on the margins,
the ones who refuse to be erased.

Every step I take is resistance,
every breath a benediction.
I walk this queer path with fire in my bones—
your love, my armor.

Forget the chains they tried to bind me with—purity, shame, fear.
I dance in liberation, in silk and steel, in the fierce truth of who I am.

God is not a straight line—
They are spiral,
They are spectrum,
They are the ache in my chest
when someone calls me beloved
and means it.

Psalm 120

I called out from the margins—
lipstick smeared, heart shattered,
my truth trembling on my tongue—and You heard me.
Not with lightning bolts or commandments, but with the quiet hum of
survival that said: *Stay. Breathe. Rise.*

Rescue me from the mouths that twist love into lies,
from tongues sharpened like knives disguised as scripture,
cutting us down while preaching "grace."
They don't know peace, only war-drum hearts
that beat to the rhythm of control.

I've lived too long as a stranger in rooms where my pronouns were jokes,
where my love was a thing to be pitied or cured.
I'm done.

Woe is me—not for being queer, but for being told I shouldn't be.
I've walked on eggshells that cracked under silence,
my own voice swallowed to keep the peace that never included me.

But no more.

They cry for war,
but I—
I am a poem of peace,
tattooed in resilience,
spilling over with the holy ache
of chosen family and freedom kisses.

Let me live, Love.
Not quietly. Not safely.
But truly.

Psalm 121

I lift my eyes from the dust, from streets that have tried to erase me, to
the skyline, to the stars, to every place my heart dared dream of—
and I ask,
Where will my help come from?

It comes from Love, not the kind wrapped in conditions or straight
lines,
but Love that made galaxies and glitter,
that carved mountains and bodies
and said,
You are good.

This Love doesn't sleep on me. They don't doze off when the world
starts shouting slurs, or when my legs shake from too many days
surviving.
No—They are awake with me in the midnight panic, in the sunrise
stumble, in the silent scream.

They don't let my foot slip. When I falter, when I question if I can keep
going in a world that sometimes wants me gone—
They steady me,
queer hands holding queer hands,
ancestors humming strength
into my skin.

They are shade when the spotlight burns,
shelter when the cold of isolation cuts deep.
No sunstroke of shame,
no moonlit fear can undo me.

They keep me, not in chains,
but in grace—
every breath, every step, held in the arms of a Love that refuses to let
me go.

Coming and going, breaking and becoming,
They are here.
Now. Always.

Beloved, we are kept.
Not because we are perfect—
but because we are.

Psalm 122

I was glad—
glad like the first time I wore clothes that felt like home,
like the first kiss that tasted like truth—when they said to me,
"Let's go to the place where all of you is welcome."

Our feet stood at the threshold of something holy,
not behind stained-glass walls of shame, but among chosen family,
on streets paved with glitter and grace,
where joy is resistance and every body is a sanctuary.

Here, the city of belonging rises—not built with conformity,
but with the hands of those who know what it means to fight for their
place.
Tribes of all colors, all pronouns, dancing in defiance, singing in
survival, gathering not because we're the same, but because Love called
us home.

We go there to remember—to center the sacred in each other's eyes,
to declare peace in queer tongues,
to pray not for tolerance, but for *liberation*.

So I whisper peace
to every trans heart bruised by violence,
to every ace soul told they're broken,
to every enby body navigating a binary world—
Peace be within you. You are whole.

For the sake of those I love—
those who have held me through dysphoria and doubt, those who've
danced beside me when the world felt heavy—I will speak:
You are beloved. You are needed. You are sacred.

And for the sake of the house of Love Herself,
whose walls are stitched with our names,
whose doors swing wide for every pilgrim heart—
I will seek good.
I will seek justice.
I will seek *you*.

Psalm 123

I lift my eyes—not to kings, not to systems, not to pulpits that silenced
me—but to You,
Divine Lover of the outcast and outrageous, Guardian of glowing
misfits, Goddess of holy resistance.

Like a drag queen watching for the mic drop, like a trans kid scanning
the sky for hope,
like lovers clinging in the storm—we look to You,
waiting, aching, for mercy
that doesn't come with conditions.

Enough. We've tasted the poison of mockery—been laughed at in locker
rooms, dismissed at family tables, called "too much,"
"not enough,"
"abomination,"
when all we ever wanted was to live *unafraid*.

Our souls have been soaked in the scorn of those who walk easy roads,
who weaponize comfort, who build towers of pride on our broken
backs.

But here we stand—eyes up,
hearts open, ready for the mercy that flows from pierced hands and
queer grace,
ready for the Love that does not turn away.

O Fierce One, wrap us in Your gaze.
Let them see that our survival is sacred.
Let them know
that our joy
is mercy unleashed.

Psalm 124

If it hadn't been for Love—
for the Divine who queers all things,
for the Fierce One who carved rainbows into the sky,
who stitched survival into our bones—we would have been erased,
flattened by systems that called us shame, buried by hands that refused
to see our light.

If Love hadn't stood with us, when power came for our names,
when laws cracked down on our bodies, when churches slammed doors
in our faces—
we would have been devoured by hate,
flooded by lies,
drowned in the silence they demanded from us.

But Love did stand.
Love rose like a riot.
Love tore down the binary walls,
spoke our pronouns into holy echoes,
and we—we slipped free,
like a bird from the hunter's trap,
wings wild,
hearts on fire.

The snare is broken.
We are not caught.
We are not gone.
We are not their shame.

Our help is in the One
who spun galaxies from star dust,
who made trans bodies holy,
who painted queerness into the dawn.

We are still here.
We rise in that Name.

Psalm 125

Those who root themselves in Love, who plant their hearts in justice,
are unshakable—
like mountains queering the skyline, fierce and unmoved, their foundations kissed by eternity.

As ancient hills rise around the city, so does the Holy surround us—
wrapping trans bodies in tenderness, enfolding queer souls in safety,
holding space for every pronoun,
every becoming.

Oppression may reign for a moment, systems may bend their weight on
backs they deem unworthy—
but Love does not forget.
Love does not let injustice hold the crown forever.

Let goodness rise in the hearts of those who rise for others.
Let peace bloom where rage and resistance have made way.

To those who weaponize faith,
who twist sacred words into blades—
your power will fall,
your grip will crumble,
for Love is not yours to hoard.

Peace upon us.
Peace upon us,
the misfits and the dreamers,
the lovers and the fighters—
we, the holy remnant,
the unyielding flame.

Psalm 126

When the Divine brought us back—drag queens, dykes, trans angels,
sacred and scattered—from exile, from closets, from silence, we were
dreamers tasting daylight for the first time.

Our mouths spilled laughter, not the polite kind, but wild, body-shak-
ing, holy laughter that tore through shame like sunrise through fog.

We sang—songs stitched from survival,
from nights we thought we wouldn't make it,
from bones that remembered how to dance even in despair.

And the world saw us and said,
"Something radiant is happening—look what Love has done."
And we, breathless with wonder, whispered back,
"Yes—look what Love has done."

Bring us back again, Holy One—not to where we were,
but forward, to the place we've never been but have always longed for—
a home built from truth, from chosen family, from boundless grace.

Let our tears—each one shed for who we lost, for who we were not
allowed to be—
soak the ground and bloom into liberation.

Those who weep now will one day return carrying joy in their arms
like harvest,
like promise,
like pride that cannot be silenced.

Psalm 127

If the Holy One isn't in it—if Love isn't the architect—
what are we even building?
Towering closets, gilded shame, cities without sanctuary?
No thanks.
I'm done laying bricks for palaces that exile me.

If we rise at dawn, grind 'til our souls are sore, but forget to rest,
forget to breathe,
forget to *be*—
we've missed the point. Even the Divine took a break. Even stars rest in
daylight.

We are not machines.
We are not only what we produce.
We are art.
We are breath.
We are divine exhale wrapped in skin.

And children—not just of blood,
but of spirit, of chosen ties—the ones who know your heart-song, who
stand beside you
when the world turns cold—they are the arrows of tomorrow, the
poetry of resistance,
the proof that love multiplies when shared.

Blessed is the one who fills their life
not with fear or toil,
but with kin,
with joy,
with purpose that cannot be stolen or sold.

For when we build with Love,
our houses stand,
our hearts sing,
and no gatekeeper can keep us out.

Psalm 128

Blessed are you, who walk in your truth—not the truth they handed you wrapped in fear and control—but the truth you forged with trembling hands and holy courage.

Blessed are you, who love in the open, who kiss without shame, who hold hands under streetlights and in sanctuaries that once shut you out.

Blessed are you, who nourish joy like a garden growing wild
—your laughter spilling over like wine, like music, like a dance that never ends.

In your home—crafted not from blueprints but from chosen family, inside jokes, and walls that echo with love's fierce echo—
there is peace,
there is abundance,
there is enough.

Your table—whether crowded with friends, solo in sacred stillness, or shared with one
who knows your scars—
overflows with blessing.

You will see good things.
You will witness joy in the hearts of your people,
the rising of your own light day by day.

And may you live long enough to see freedom unfold in the lives of those who come after—
our queerlings,
our kin,
the ones who know that love is holy,
and understand that every heart deserves to be at rest.

PSALM 129

They've tried to silence us since the first breath we dared to take,
since we danced in colors they couldn't name
and loved in ways they tried to erase.

Since our beginnings, we've been scarred,
plowed deep by hatred's hand—
but we are still here.
Still alive.
Still rising.

The world carved wounds into our backs—
laws, slurs, fists,
conversion prayers,
disowned dinners,
empty chairs at family tables.
But we did not fall.
Queer joy outlasted every blow.

Let those who hate us vanish like mist in the morning,
shrivel like grass trapped under concrete,
never to thrive,
never to suffocate us again.

Let them not be blessed with the power to define us.
Let no one look at their hate and call it holy.

We are not waiting for their approval,
not begging for space at their table.

We have built our own feast.
We have danced in the rain.
We have kissed under stars that do not judge.

We are the blessing.
We are the survivors.
We are the dream they couldn't kill.

Psalm 130

From the depths, I speak.
Not in whispers, but in the full, fierce sound of a soul unhidden.

I have known darkness, not as an absence of light, but as a refusal—
the world refusing to see me as beloved,
refusing to hear my name without twisting it into something they
could use.

I have waited, not with idle hands,
but with hands that held the weight of being
misunderstood,
misgendered,
misloved.
And still, I wait for grace that does not come with conditions.

If grace were a ledger, who could stand?
Not one.
Not one without cracks, without shame hidden beneath buttoned-up
faith.
But grace is not a tally of rights and wrongs—
it is the breath we take when we dare to live out loud.

I wait, but not in silence.
I wait with the cry of my people in my chest, with the pulse of queer
ancestors in my veins.
I wait with hope, as radical as it is tender, as daring as it is deserved.

Let the people know:
We are not a problem to be solved, but a promise to be kept.

Let love be the answer we no longer question.
Let redemption come not as a rescue but as a recognition:
We were never wrong to be who we are.

We rise from the depths, and we do not rise alone.

Psalm 131

I have stopped chasing approval like it's oxygen.
Stopped trying to climb every ladder they built to keep me out.

My heart—
it no longer beats to the rhythm of who I'm supposed to be.
It slows,
softens,
settles into itself.

I do not need to be grand,
or loud,
or in control of every moment.
It is enough to exist in this body,
on this day,
with breath in my lungs
and love in my bones.

I have unlearned the need to prove myself to a world that cannot
hold me.

Like a child resting in arms that do not flinch, I rest.
Not because I have all the answers, but because I am finally okay with
not needing them.

Hope doesn't have to be a battle cry.
Sometimes it's just a quiet knowing that we belong
without question,
without condition,
without apology.

We—
the ones who were told we were too much,
too little,
too different—
we hope,
and in that hope,
we are free.

Psalm 132

Remember us—not as myths, but as makers.
Not as broken, but as builders.

We have sworn oaths not to kings, but to kindness.
Not to thrones, but to truth that fits
in every heart,
in every body, without borders.

We searched for sanctuary not in gold-plated temples,
but in each other—
in back-alley promises and front-porch laughter,
in the way we hold an expansive space when the world tries to eradicate
us.

We said:
We will not rest until home exists for every single soul who has been told
they are unworthy of one.

And the Divine—
She heard. They saw. He came close
like breath,
like protest,
like love that refuses to let go.

God did not choose palaces of power—
God chose
the trembling hand,
the weary marcher,
the ones whose names were never spoken on the news but carved in
heaven.

From our stories, God built a dwelling.
From our survival, God crowned us not with might, but with mercy.

In every meal shared in secret,
in every dance under stars we claimed as ours,
God said:
Here I am. And we, the called and cast-aside, became the cornerstone of
a new kingdom,
not ruled,
but risen.

We are not waiting to be welcomed.
We are building a forever in the ruins of rejection.

Psalm 133

How holy, how breathtaking, when we come together
not by blood, but by bond.
Not by lineage, but by love chosen
again
and again
and again.

Unity—not the kind that demands we all look the same,
but the kind that celebrates the mosaic of us:
scars and sparkle,
freedom and fire.

It's like glitter spilled on the earth—
unexpected, radiant, impossible to clean up.
It clings to everything, refuses to fade.

It's like balm on bruised skin,
like laughter that shows up just when grief tried to stay the night.

This—this gathering of souls who refused to vanish—
this is sacred.
This is oil on the head of the weary, running down into the cracks we
thought made us weak but turned out to be where the light gets in.

This is blessing.
This is breath.
This is the pulse of forever—
not promised to the powerful,
but poured out on the people who dared to hold each other
close enough to be called kin.

PSALM 134

Hey you,
the ones still standing when the world sleeps—
hands blistered, hearts burning, souls humming midnight hymns in
sacred defiance—
lift your voice.

You who tend the flame when no one else sees it.
You who stitch joy into the shadows.
You who dance on the edge of exhaustion and call it worship—
you are the altar.

Lift your hands, tattoos and tremors and all.
Let your prayers be loud, even if they tremble.
Let your breath be the incense,
your existence the offering.

Bless the Source who never sleeps on you.
Bless the Mystery who knows your name before you dare say it aloud.

And may that same wild Love pour blessing over you
from the mountaintops to the back alleys,
from holy ground to hospital floor,
from drag stage to sanctuary—
because you,
yes you,
are worthy of it all.

Psalm 135

Hey beloveds, chosen kin, sacred misfits and holy rebels—
shout praise, not quiet like a whisper
but bold like a parade in June or a protest in the rain.

Sing to the Source who carved queerness into the cosmos,
who inked resistance into your DNA.
Praise them in the glow of glitter and grief, in the ache of becoming,
in the joy of surviving when survival was never promised.

We know this: Our God, our Love, our ever-expanding Universe
is not small or cis or straight—
They are vast, wild, fierce with compassion, tender with rage.

They make art out of chaos,
pull beauty from the margins.
They don't sit on thrones—they march in the streets,
cry in our arms,
laugh in our beds,
call pronouns holy
and names sacred.

They cracked the systems—broke open the binaries,
shattered the idols of power.
Let the gods of oppression tremble,
let the machines of empire crumble—we do not bow to injustice.

Let every breath be a banner.
Let every step be a hymn.
Let every queer body be a temple that colonizers can't colonize and
churches can't erase.

O house of resistance, bless them.
O house of chosen kin, lift them up.
O house of holy queers, shine like the fire you are.

Bless the One who sees you, knows you, loves you—
exactly as you are, and exactly as you will be.

Psalm 136

Give it up for the One who queered the stars into being, for the Artist of the galaxies, the Dreamer of pronouns and possibilities—
Their love endures, and so do we.

For the Breath that hovered over chaos, that kissed void into sunrise, that called every "too much" and "not enough" beloved—

Their love endures, and so do we.
To the One who stitched every color into rainbows and revolutions, who made glitter a weapon and softness a shield—
Their love endures, and so do we.

They cracked open binaries with holy hands, dismantled every empire that tried to legislate love—
Their love endures, and so do we.

When they led us out of closets and cages, through deserts of silence, into streets echoing with chants—
Their love endures, and so do we.

To the One who fed us when the world withheld, who carved altars out of park benches, and lit candles in bathrooms when safety was a myth—
Their love endures, and so do we.

When our names were erased, they wrote them on the sky. When our bodies were shamed, they crowned them sacred. When our loves were outlawed, they sanctified our kisses—
Their love endures, and so do we.

They remember every ancestor who dared to love out loud, who danced when told to hide, who built homes with chosen family—
Their love endures, and so do we.

To the One who fights beside us, marches with us, weeps and laughs and refuses to quit—
Their love endures, and so do we.

O holy fire that can't be doused, O fierce embrace that never lets go—
Their love endures, and so do we.
Their love endures, and so do we.
Their love endures, and so—do—we.

Psalm 137

By the rivers of those who forgot our names, we sat down in silence, and
the weight of our grief bent us low.
We hung up our songs on the branches of trees that never offered shade,
in cities that took our voices and called it law.

They asked us for celebration while building monuments on our pain.
"Sing us a song," they said, "of joy, of praise, of your God."
But how can we sing when our tongues are swollen with sorrow, when
our hands tremble from holding too much?

They erased the place we called home—not just land,
but the space inside our bodies where we once felt safe, where we danced
without shame, where our love was never labeled wrong.

O memory, if I forget who I am, if I betray the sacredness of my own
skin, may my voice falter, may my hands forget their strength.
Let me remember the holy ground I walk on—
my own truth,
my own breath,
the divine dwelling in my queerness.

Blessed are those who refuse to bow to the powers that exile,
who gather in secret,
who love in the open,
who rise again and again.

And for those who built their joy on the backs of our silence—
know this:
we will tear down your golden lies.
We will cradle the cries of our wounded
until they rise into anthem,
until no child is left shattered on the altars of your fear.

By the rivers of rage and hope,
we rise.
We rebuild our songs.
We carry each other home.

Psalm 138

I give thanks with every shade of who I am—no more dimming,
no more shrinking to fit the silence of others.
I lay my praise loud before the Divine, who met me in the closet,
held me on the bathroom floor, and whispered,
"You are holy, as you are."

No god of power, no throne of gold ever offered what You did—
the unshakable truth:
I was made from stardust and defiance, from tenderness and fire.
And I will not bow to fear wearing a crown.

When I called out in my trembling, You answered with thunder.
Not to frighten, but to remind me—my voice has weight.
My story is storm-born. You made me brave when I only wanted to
disappear.

Let the mighty hear this anthem and tremble—not in fear, but in awe of
a love that cannot be erased.
Even in all their glory, they never knew the kind of power it takes to live
out loud in a world that dares you to vanish.

You walk with me, not ahead or behind, but beside—
when the road is paved with slurs, with rejections, with broken glass
masquerading as acceptance.
Your hands—calloused and real—lift me.
Steady me.

When others tried to unmake me, Your love wove me tighter.
You didn't just see my scars—You saw through them, into the sacred
rage, the gentle mercy that fuels every breath I take.

You will not abandon what You created in love.
You will finish this revolution in me, in us—queer and beloved.
Your love outlasts the hate.
Your truth outshines their lies.
Forever.
Unashamed.

Psalm 139

You've explored every part of me, Radiant Spirit, and you know me in all my queer glory. You see me in my closetedness, in my 'passing' nature, in my fear of self-expression AND in my flamboyance, in my authenticity, in my joy; you sense my thoughts, no matter how wild. YOU...get me, every fabulous inch; you're familiar with all my ways. Before a word leaves my lips, you already know it in its full, vibrant truth.

You surround me with your fierce love, and you hold me close with tender care. Such wisdom is beyond me, so wondrous, so validating that I cannot grasp it.

Where can I escape your glittering presence? Where can I hide from your divine embrace? If I open myself to an inclusive embodiment of joy, you're there; if I plunge into the depths of sorrow and confinement, you're there too. If I ride the rainbow to the ends of the earth, or dance on the farthest shores, even there, your hand will guide me, your love will hold me fierce and fabulous.

If I think, "Surely the shadows will hide me, and the light around me will turn dark," even the shadows are not dark to you; the night blazes like the day, for darkness is as radiant as light to you.

You crafted my innermost being; you stitched me together with love and pride. I celebrate you because I am fearfully and wonderfully queer; your works are magnificent, and my soul revels in this truth, even when it's a challenge to believe it and especially when others protest against it.

My form was never hidden from you when I was created in secret, intricately woven in the depths of mystery. Your eyes saw my unformed essence. How precious are your thoughts of me, Radiant Spirit, more than vitriol in every single troll comment on the internet that would tell me otherwise!

If only you, Radiant Spirit, would rid the world of bigotry! Alas it is I who must learn the words 'Away from me, you who spread hate'! They drag your name through the mud but we will reclaim the power of

Drag. We oppose them with every fiber of our being and continue to proclaim boldly the expansiveness of your love in and through all flesh. Search each of us, Radiant Spirit, and know our hearts; know my wildest dreams and lead us in the way of eternal pride.

Amen.

Psalm 140

Rescue me, Divine Beloved, from those who wield power like a blade—
those who twist words into weapons, who grind peace to dust beneath
polished shoes.

They plot in boardrooms, in back pews, behind closed doors
with clenched fists and fake smiles.
Their tongues spit venom—and they call it *righteousness.*
They craft laws like shackles, pray for purity while stoking hate.

But You, O Flame that cannot be tamed, You are my refuge—
my sanctuary in the crossfire. You know the ache of being othered, the
bruise of being seen as threat instead of wonder.

Do not let the wicked write my story.
Let their traps collapse beneath them.
Let the nets they weave ensnare their own hypocrisy.
Let the justice they deny rise like a flood and wash them bare.

I know You see me—see us—all of us stitched from stardust and
survival,
from glitter and grief, from kisses shared in secret and battles fought in
daylight.

You will not forget the cry of the misfit,
the song of the exiled,
the tears of the resilient.
You will not ignore the way we rise,
refusing to be erased.

Surely the Beloved sides with the fierce, defends the tender-hearted, a
home for the outcast in the very place they were cast out.

So we stand.
Still here.
Still holy.
Still held.

Psalm 141

Beloved, I call to You—not in whispers,
but in a voice honed by longing,
by dance floors and protests,
by kitchen tables where chosen families gather and love defies
expectation.

Rush to me—like a song I didn't know I needed
until the bass hit my ribcage and shook loose my fear.

Let my prayer rise before You like incense in the drag of night,
my hands lifted up like candles flickering in defiance of darkness,
in worship of truth and survival.

Set a guard over my lips—not to silence, but to sanctify.
Let my words sparkle with grace, cut with clarity, never wielded to harm
but always to heal, to stir the sleeping, to soothe the weary.

Keep my soul from the snares—the false sanctity of respectability,
the trap of self-erasure, the glowing lure of fitting in when I was made to
stand out in holy hues.

Let me not feast at the table of the arrogant, where love is conditional,
and bodies are policed into shame.

Let the fierce ones correct me in love—
the queer elders, the radical dreamers,
the ones who've wept and risen a thousand times over.

Their words are balm, not bruises—truth spoken to remind me who I
am when the world tries to rewrite me.

My eyes are set on You, O Holy Disruptor—
my shelter, my spark, my wild and wondrous muse.
Do not leave me to the machines of hate.

Let me walk through the fire unscathed in spirit, cloaked in all my
queerness, holy and whole and absolutely unafraid.

PSALM 142

I cry aloud to You,
Beloved of the outcast and the bold. I speak Your name like a protest
chant echoing off walls, a litany of survival in a world that keeps trying
to erase me.

I pour out my story before You—raw,
unedited, a litany of scars and small victories, a confession not of sin but
of being tired, worn, yet still burning.

When my spirit falters—when the weight of closets, church pews that
don't want me, bathrooms that feel like battlegrounds, and family
dinners soaked in silence press against my ribs like a vice—You know.

You see the maze I walk, the ways I contort to stay safe, to stay seen, to
stay me.

They've set traps, called me
"too much,"
"not enough,"
"abomination,"
"confusion."
They weaponize scripture as if Your love were ever a tool for harm.

Look—I'm alone again. Chosen family scattered. My phone silent. No
refuge in sight. No one who truly knows how the ache sings when I
stand in a room and still feel invisible.

So I call to You, my sanctuary, my holy refuge when the world bars the
door.

Hear me. I am down to embers—
my power,
my dignity,
threatened but not gone.

Rescue me from the shadows, from those who fear what they don't understand, who hate what they cannot control.

Bring me back into the light of queer kinship, of sacred resistance, of being fully and unapologetically -- alive.

Then—I will rise.
And the liberated ones will gather, dancing with me,
our joy a thunderclap.
We will tell the story of how You never abandoned us. How You crowned our grief with glory. How You made the cave a cathedral and our survival a song of praise.

Psalm 143

Listen, Beloved—not with judgment but with the tenderness of someone who's seen all the times I've been torn apart and still chose to breathe.

Don't weigh my worth by the rules they wrote to control us. No one could stand straight under that kind of weight. I'm not here to be perfect—I'm here to be real.

The world feels like it's closing in again. My enemies wear suits, pulpits, hashtags. Their weapons are laws, slurs, "prayers for my soul," like salvation is a leash.

I'm tired, God. My bones hum with exhaustion, my heart is dust where hope used to live.

I remember—when I was young, before I knew they'd try to erase me. I remember how it felt to believe You loved me as I was—no need to hide, no need to fight just to exist.

Now I stretch out my hands like branches after a storm, begging light, water, something to fill the emptiness.

Answer me soon—this silence is heavy. Don't let despair be louder than You.
Let me hear Your love before the world swallows what's left of me.

Point me toward safety—not safety as in silence, but safety in being fully seen,
held, free.

Teach me to walk again, not in their footsteps but on the path where I can breathe,
create, love without fear.

My life is Yours—not theirs.
I give it to You, not to be used, but to be lifted,
to burn with the purpose You breathed into me.

Break the grip of those who hate me.
You are my refuge, not their laws, not their churches, not their fragile power.

Let Your spirit—wild, queer, uncontainable—lead me into the open.
Let justice rise with me. Let mercy walk beside me.

For Your name—for Your love—for all the queers crying out at midnight—bring us through.

Alive.
Unashamed.
Unbroken.

Psalm 144

Blessed be the One who teaches my hands to build,
my voice to rise, my love to be a weapon against the fear they call holy.

You are my rock, but not the kind they've thrown at me.
You are my refuge, but not the closet they forced me into.
You are the breath in my lungs when the world tries to choke the truth
from me.

What are we, O God, that You are mindful of us?
That You would bend so low to whisper love into the bodies they tried
to erase?
We are mist, they say—gone too soon,
unwanted,
forgotten.

But You—You send fire from the heavens. You shake the earth when
injustice reigns.
You reach down into the depths of our grief and pull us out.

Rescue us from the hands of those who use Your name to sharpen their
swords.
Deliver us from the mouths that call us unnatural, while their own
hearts are stone.

Let a new song rise—not one of fear, but of freedom.
Let our voices ring out in sanctuaries and streets,
in bedrooms and basements,
in the arms of lovers and the laughter of friends.

Make us strong, not in violence, but in truth.
Let the next generation inherit joy, not shame—homes where they are
held, futures where they can flourish.

Let our harvest be justice, our fields full of kindness, our streets safe for
every body that dares to dance in the daylight.

Blessed are the people who refuse to be erased.
Blessed are the ones who know that Love was never meant
to be a cage.

Psalm 145

I will bless the Holy One with every breath I take,
with every part of me that was never meant to be hidden.
I will speak Her name
the way I was told not to—with pride,
with tenderness,
with fire in my bones.

Generations will tell the story
of how Love refused to bow to empire,
how She showed up in the margins,
how She carved a path
for those the world discarded.

The Holy One is vast beyond measure,
Her greatness spilling over
into places they never expected to find Her.
Her kindness is fierce,
Her mercy relentless—not just for some,
but for all.

She lifts the ones who were trampled underfoot,
the ones the church abandoned,
the ones who prayed for a miracle
and found it in themselves.

The Holy One is near
to those who call out in truth—
not in fear,
not in shame,
but in the fullness
of their own becoming.

She sees us.
She hears us.
She delights in us.

Let every voice,
every body,
every story they tried to erase
sing praise.

PSALM 146

Praise the Holy One!
Praise the Love that refuses to die!
I will not waste my breath
on kings who never spoke my name,
on leaders who built walls
instead of open doors.
Their reigns crumble.
Their promises fade.
Their justice is a whisper
drowned out by sirens.

But the Divine—
Oh, the Divine is a revolution.
God is the One who walks into the locked room,
who rolls away every stone,
who lifts the broken, the burdened, the bent,
and says, "Stand up."

The Creator does not check IDs at the gates of grace.
She feeds the hungry—
even the ones they said weren't worthy.
They said I wasn't worthy,
but still, Love put food on my table.
They said I was an abomination,
but still, Love set me free.

The Holy One sets the prisoners loose,
opens the eyes of those
who have only known the dark,
raises those crushed
beneath the weight of the world.
The Eternal watches over the exiles,
holds close the abandoned,
and cradles the lost.

Let the wicked tremble.
Let the oppressors scatter.
Love reigns forever.

Psalm 147

Sing praise to the One
who stitches the world back together!
Who gathers up the scattered,
who builds a home out of the broken.

God is the One
who holds the survivor's shaking hands,
who sits with the exile in the night,
who binds up wounds that churches ignored.

God does not delight in the strong man's sword,
or in the banners of those who conquer,
but in the quiet endurance
of the ones who refused to stay hidden,
in the courage of those
who dared to be soft
when the world demanded armor.

Praise the One who opens the skies,
who sends down rain
on lands that were barren,
on hearts that were closed.

God has never needed empire to bring justice.
She speaks through the mouths of the silenced.
She sings in the voices of those
who were never supposed to survive.

Hallelujah to the ones who are still here.

Psalm 148

Praise the Holy One,
from the heavens and the deep.
Praise Her in every language,
in every accent,
with every name
they told us was too much.

Praise Her,
sun, moon, and neon lights.
Praise Her,
fire escapes and drag stages,
bedroom mirrors where we first met our own reflection.

Let every body rise
and give thanks—
the bodies that fit,
and the bodies that never did.
The ones they tried to erase,
the ones they tried to fix,
the ones that shine
in all their transfigured glory.

Praise the Holy One,
who calls us very good,
who makes no mistakes,
who has never required
anyone to shrink to be saved.

Let the stars clap their hands,
let the trees wave their arms,
let the queer ones dance
like we were made for joy.
Because we were.

Psalm 149

Sing a new song—
one they cannot turn into a weapon.
Let praise rise up,
louder than the voices
that once told us to hush.

Let the march be music.
Let the banner be hymn.
Let the love between us
be the kind of worship
that shakes the heavens.

The Holy One takes delight in Her people—
not just the ones they put in the pews,
but the ones in the back alleys,
in the nightclubs,
in the places they said
She would never be.

Let the faithful rise with fire in their feet.
Let them hold hands in the streets
without fear,
without shame.

This is the honor of the beloved.
This is the song that sets us free.

Hallelujah.

Psalm 150

Praise the Holy One
in the sanctuary of the streets,
in the sacred spaces
they tried to shut us out of.
Praise Her with the bass drum
of a heartbeat that refused to still.

Praise Her with the sound of laughter
in rooms where we can finally be ourselves.
Praise Her with the clapping hands
of ballroom queens and leather dykes,
of trans elders and chosen siblings.

Let the tambourine shake like a riot.
Let the organ swell like a coming-out song.
Let the drag queens and the choir kids
join in the same refrain.

Let everything that breathes—
everything that has ever been called unholy,
everything that has ever been cast out—
let it all
praise the Holy One.

Hallelujah.